THE TEST OF TIME

The Test of Time

What Makes a Classic a Classic?

edited by Andrew Holgate and

Honor Wilson-Fletcher

A W Magazine Publication
Published in association with
The Arts Council of England

First published in Great Britain in 1999
by Waterstone's, Capital Court
Capital Interchange Way
Brentford, Middlesex TW8 0EX

© Waterstone's Booksellers 1999

A CIP catalogue record for this book is available from the British Library.

ISBN 1 902603 08 7

Typeset in New Baskerville by Parker Typesetting, Leicester

Printed and bound by CPD Wales

Contents

Foreword

by Andrew Holgate and
Honor Wilson-Fletcher

Any bookseller could (and will, given half a chance) regale you with accounts of debates, wrangles and minor fist fights about the appropriate 'home' for certain books in a store. The function of a bookshop is to arrange as many books as possible in as logical a fashion as possible to make them as easy to find as possible. The whole issue of how to shelve 'the classic' most appropriately is one of the most contentious of the 'categorisation wars', and in addition suffers from the potentially unpleasant aroma of snobbery and elitism. Aren't classics, after all, just stuffy collections of inpenetrable prose written by academics at some point in the fairly distant past? (Either that or nineteenth-century soap operas only repopularised by television?) Is it neccessary to have a 'classics' section in a bookshop? Is it helpful, or merely confusing? Aren't we somehow beyond all that now, in a moderated age of equal rights for all books, irrespective of heritage?

Even if we do want to single out books of particular distinction, what criteria should we use? Does anyone have a better name for great books, or a way of identifying them, than that of 'The Classic'? This is the really substantial debate – the nature, status and relevance of the classic today. Many of the contributors to this book really dislike the idea of 'classics', but show remarkable accord in their interpretations of what makes a 'special' or perennially good book. As Lawrence Norfolk puts it, 'The historical wave is the one to ride.' Time may not be a perfect filter, but it seems to have worked remarkably well thus far.

Here, then, is the kernel of the idea that became this book, and which filled the Arts Council of England with sufficient enthusiasm to wish to join in. It was an opportunity to gauge the opinions of experts authors, poets, editors and publishers of both books and newspapers, and key individuals in the public sector with a stake in the Arts, on just this subject – what makes a classic a classic? Their responses offer a great spectrum of ideas and it seems reasonable to speculate that every reader will come across at least one set of answers with which they will violently disagree. There is still a debate to be had, it seems.

The publication of this book gives Waterstone's the chance to celebrate a tremendous range of titles which the contributors to this collection have nominated as essential reading well into the twenty-first century. (Explore the lists at the end of the book to see if you agree with their choices.) Importantly, the book itself is a very enjoyable read – this seems to be a frequent test for the books our contributors have nominated too. Not just respected and admired, their contributed titles are loved. It's an appealing definition; a classic as a piece of writing that lasts, and continues to be well-loved by generations of readers. But ultimately the definition of a classic has to be about recognising quality. It is good to try and point out the very, very best writing and to celebrate it as loudly as possible – 'classic' may not be the best badge for a book to wear, and may well carry a faint whiff of the classroom with it, but it has to be important for us to recognise and treasure serious talent in contemporary writing, and to continually trawl our heritage of authorship to ensure that less widely celebrated works do not get forgotten.

Let's face it, all books are not great, and with over a million currently in print in this country, we could all occasionally do with some original and inspired guidance. This book carries with it the combined authority of some of our best writers and editors, and should form a pretty reliable guide for anyone in search of help. It also draws attention to some of the 'quieter' books that may already have slipped out of print for the want of a little more attention.

At the end of this book is an astonishing reading list for anyone with the energy to take it on. That alone made publishing this book worthwhile. It's a memorable celebration of great writing in every possible form. The ideas in many of these books continue to challenge our understanding and philosophical approach to ourselves and the Universe around us. We have been producing memorable writing throughout history, and a considerable amount of it (whatever we decide to call it) continues to be both exciting and relevant. It seems encouragingly likely that writing from the last thousand years will still have much to contribute to the enjoyment, comfort and understanding of readers in the twenty-first century.

Waterstone's would like to thank all those who agreed to take part in this project, and in particular Gary McKeone of the Arts Council of England. Gary's passion for the celebration of writing, and his loathing of redundant snobbery and outdated or lazy thinking, makes him enormous fun to work with. And he's read a good book or two too.

Introduction

by John Sutherland

For the book buyer with a reflective turn of mind the 1990's are exciting times. After decades of apocalypticism about the death of the book (in which, I confess, I have done my share of doom-crying) that most indestructible of inventions thrives as never before. Transport William Caxton back to the future in a time machine and the West End streets would be a nightmare of strangeness. He would be like Craig Raine's Martian: goggle-eyed at the young people clutching mobiles to their heads and talking to themselves (a new version of the leper's clapper, perhaps?). He would cringe at the smoke-belching horseless carriages; he would be gobsmacked by the talking and flashing black boxes in shop-windows.

But one thing would be comfortingly familiar – the overflowing content of the many bookstores. As he browsed, Master Caxton would pause a minute or two on the dustjackets, title pages, and page-numbers (why hadn't he thought of those?). But the book *qua* book would strike him as essentially the same object that he himself made and sold in his fifteenth-century shop. Caxton could easily reproduce Tom Wolfe's *A Man in Full* using his medieval technology. To his delight, Caxton would discover two of his titles in the shop's 'classics' section – Chaucer's *Canterbury Tales* and Malory's *Morte d'Arthur*. Five hundred years, and still selling! ('But what kind of bird, pray, is a "Penguin"? Phoenixes I've heard of.')

There is something wonderful about the new-born perfection of the codex book in the late fifteenth century and its cultural longevity as a receptacle for the products of the human mind. It's like the Eskimo igloo. One can't see how it could be improved (don't tell me about Palm Pilots – they're a big pain in the arm, they cost too much and they don't work).

In my lifetime, other such receptacles have mutated faster than fruit-flies. TV has gone from 8-inch black-and-white to remote controlled 26-inch colour, with digital on the way. One scarcely gets the new set out of its packing case before it's obsolete. As an adolescent I bought shellac 10-inch 78rpm records and played them on a 'wind-up', clockwork-powered portable (this was the 1950's). Within a couple of years, I had vinyl EPs and LPs and an electric turntable. In the early 1960's I bought a Grundig tape recorder about the size of a small Wurlitzer (and about as complicated to operate) and a 'Hi-Fi' complete with woofers and tweeters. So it goes. Just for the irony of it, I'm playing the first record I ever bought (Vogue Records 78, Earl Bostic's 'Flamingo', 6/-) in its CD version, on the stereo system built into my computer. As I listen, I can see on my bookshelves Penguin books I bought about the same time (2/6d), which look exactly like the books on sale in the local bookshop. They haven't changed a bit (except for the pictorial covers, the price and the disappearance of the lovely half-crown coin).

Alan Turing, the inventor of the modern computer, pointed out that as an information storage device the book has it over both the papyrus scroll (which the codex book replaced) and the RAM/ROM systems on which today's PC operates. The reasoning is complex but boils down to the following. The advantage of books is that, if you need something on page 259, you don't have to turn over 258 pages to get there; you cut in, using opposable thumb and eye, roughly to where you want to be and refine your search from there. As intact packages, books can be arranged by catalogue so you know where to look for the book that contains the information you need. Computers find these deceptively primitive search and locate operations very difficult to emulate. They haven't, thank God, yet cracked it.

There is something emotionally reassuring about books. Some pre-industrial things last, they tell us. This, as it happens, is the motif which Waterstone's has chosen to stress in its marketing operations. Go into a 'Big W' and what you enter is a kind of mini-cathedral dedicated to the book as timeless icon. It's a consciously different marketing strategy from that currently being imported from the US by Border's Inc. Their trick is to 'bland down' the book ('desacralise' it, as we used to say in our hot Marxist youth). You go into Border's, buy a paper, buy a coffee and Danish, buy a book – no difference. There's nothing special about these bundles of printed materials. Books? No big deal – do you want cream with that? It will be interesting to see which of the two strategies – reverencing books or normalising them – works better.

The annual production of the book trade is now, literally, mind-boggling. A couple of years ago, Britain went through the 100,000-titles-a-year barrier. There was a time in recorded history when a 'well-read man' (unfortunately women didn't qualify) might presume to read virtually everything printed in a year. Well into the twentieth century, you could probably cover most of what was published in 'your field', without strain. What does it mean in the 1990's to be a well-read man or woman? To have read, say, one per cent of the books in one's field? Booker judges, as a measure, are expected to read 0.5 per cent of the new novels published annually (and invariably write newspaper articles about their 'Herculean' feat and how it has disrupted their lives).

There is a comfortingly solid nucleus within this inundating flux of book production – the 'classic'. These are books which (as most respondents in this round-up note) perform that most difficult of literary tricks – they work for two or more generations of readers. In so doing they become what Matthew Arnold called 'touchstones' – miniature embodiments of the best that our culture can produce; advertisements for ourselves, as Norman Mailer would say.

No one knows better than a professor of literature the sterility of critical terminology. With shrewd good sense the respondents here have generally avoided trying to define, in any conceptual way, what a classic is. They have, instead, applied two pragmatic rules of thumb. One is the 'Reader's Digest Test' ('The book(s) that changed my life'). The other is the 'Desert Island Discs Test' ('Excluding the Bible and Shakespeare, what ten books would you take with you to your island?'). A third test can be deduced from the drift of the answers: what books of my time (or my ancestors' time) would I want my children, or my contemporaries' children, to read?

In an introduction one can attempt what the respondents wisely side-step. What, then, is a 'classic'? Manageability is clearly a principal criterion in making up the category. In its narrowest sense the 'classics' are works in Latin and Greek. Classic literature thus defined, like the 'dead' classic language in which it is written, is inert and finite. There is a fixed quantum which will never grow larger. More importantly, the fragment which has descended to us is a manageable corpus. The surviving literature of ancient Greece and Rome can be contained on two 3.5-inch 'floppies' and an undergraduate curriculum.

Look at the 1998–9 Penguin Classics and World's Classics catalogues. They comprise some 600 titles apiece (predominantly novels). In sum, this is just about what one could manage in an average reading career. What the 'classic' category does, then, is to reduce the unimaginably vast production of two-millennia's worth of literature into a portable package equivalent to the dimensions of the surviving literature of Greece and Rome. One cannot see the end of 'the English novel'; there are some 4,000 (new and reprints) published every year. As well count the pebbles on the sea shore. But one can master the classics of our fiction. Arguably, every cultivated person should.

There is, of course, more to the idea of the classic than logistics. The modern critic who has thought most productively about the nature of classics, Frank Kermode, applies two tests. The first is what he calls 'textual patience'. By this he means the paradoxical fact that every generation re-interprets a classic writer like Dickens to its own satisfaction, but differently from its predecessors. Yet no generation can say it has interpreted Dickens fully – 'solved' him, that is, as one might complete a crossword puzzle or Fermat's theorem.

Secondly, Kermode proposes, the classic should derive from a great civilisation or 'imperium'. South American banana republics or statelets like Luxembourg do not qualify. They don't have the cultural infrastructure to produce classic literature (soccer, perhaps). More debatable is Saul Bellow's grossly Eurocentric question, 'Where is the Zulu Tolstoy?' The pre-colonial civilisations of Africa may well have produced something equivalent to Homer (pre-colonial Asia demonstrably did).

As one ranges over the contents of the catalogues, one is driven to ask how this small clump of islands in the Northern seas produced such a wealth of classic literature? Britain, if one has to be honest about it, lags well behind great Continental states (Germany, France, Italy, Spain) in music, architecture and fine art (in which even tiny Belgium – Flanders – is streets ahead). Why do we do so well in literature?

The answer, I suspect, is to be found in our old friend Caxton. He was, if truth must be told, a rather mediocre maker of books compared to Gutenberg or Aldus Manutius. Nor was he, bibliographers agree, a pioneer technically. But Caxton did one exceptional thing. Unlike his Continental counterparts he published the bulk of his books in the vernacular English tongue. This boost to native speech, which can be traced from Caxton and Gower, through Spenser to Milton and Shakespeare, gave England a head start in its own national literature. The rise of the novel, with Defoe in the eighteenth century, coincided with another formative event: the growth to world power of British mercantilism. With the novel, literature became a commodity, dependent on the evolution of modern capitalism in which (up to the twentieth century) Britain was central. Add the boost to freedom of expression which came with the Reformation, and you have the makings of a classic literature.

This relates to a perceptible feature in the attached responses. As a general rule the younger the respondent, the more likely they are to include American (or in some cases, South and Central American) titles in their top-ten classics. This, gloomily, charts a decline in Britain as a cultural imperium. When the first American bestseller list was compiled, in 1896, eight out of the ten top novels were English in origin. As I write, 102 years later, the *Sunday Times* shows almost exactly the reverse: six out of the top ten novels are American. As bestsellers go, so do classics. To be ultra-gloomy, it's not far-fetched to suppose that our 'classics industry' may go the same way as British car-makers. As the second millennium proceeds, the 'English classic novel' may be as nostalgic a conception as the Humber Super Snipe, 'E'-type Jaguar or Lagonda drophead tourer. Possibly the most prognostic of the responses here is that by Tim Pears, whose 'ten best' contains not one *echt* English author (I mean no disrespect to Louis de Bernières – who surely belongs, with Marquez, Borges and Fuentes, to the South American literary tradition – or Salman Rushdie).

Most of the respondents assume that the corpus of classic texts is not fixed but alters according to historical circumstance and personal preference. Probably there is only one North Star, stationary in the wheeling classic firmament – Shakespeare. And, ominously, there are now colleges in the United States where you can get a degree in English without ever having read one of the thirty-nine plays.

Although classics are subject to the accidents of history and vagaries of taste, most respondents agree (except for wilful contra-rians like Julie Burchill) that behind these texts is 'authority'. Some older authority is Oedipally repudiated – notably in the case of Sir Walter Scott. The Great Unknown seems destined to return to the oblivion from which he emerged in 1814.

Other authorities have emerged, to elevate new texts to classic status. Feminism and post-colonialism, notably. Virginia Woolf, Jane Austen, the Brontës and Salman Rushdie all crop up time and again. (The austerely highbrow Alain de Botton is, I think, almost unique in having neither a woman nor Rushdie in his lists of ten on either side). This is, I think, less an index of enlightenment than the 'muscle' of these two constituencies. I personally regret that none of the Caribbean novelists (true glories of our literature) have made it. But I would guess that in 2099, these new flavours (and others) will predominate in any similar poll. I may say that I'm surprised that Toni Morrison seems to have missed out. We won't have to wait a century to have that put right.

No one, I think, will read this most entertaining set of responses for what they tell us about the nature of the classic. Books are the most effective of Rohrschach tests. Go into someone's house and you find a window into their soul through the bookshelves. The titles chosen by these interesting people are interestingly sometimes indiscreetly self-revealing.

Not surprisingly, publishers like Stuart Proffitt and John Calder have a soft spot for their published offspring. One reads the list of writers like Brink and Ballard (whose *Crash* would be in my list) with the covert aim of discovering what makes them tick as writers – few surprises, except for Ballard's Lawrence Durrell, an inclusion that sets the brain whirring. Academics like Tom Paulin and Richard Hoggart can't help laying down the law (although, interestingly, Hoggart's cynosure, D. H. Lawrence, turns up on quite a few thumbs-down selections). Chris Woodhead, as befits an officer with responsibility for 'standards', seems to be telling us the books we ought to read (how I would like to set him a quiz on Tolstoy and then give him feedback). Only the magnificent Burchill has the chutzpah to include one of her own works (*Ambition* – 'best novel about the Eighties ever written'; what about *Bonfire of the Vanities, Money, American Psycho, Bright Lights, Big City*, Julie?).

Hovering largely unstated over these selections is the biggest and most vexing question of all. These books are all of them, however diverse the choices, products of high civilisation. Does it therefore make us highly civilised to read them? The critic who has wrestled most conscientiously with this problem is George Steiner. His conclusion? 'We do not know – and surely there is something rather terrible in our doubt – whether the study and delight a man takes in Shakespeare makes him any less capable of organising a concentration camp.' Or Woolf, Dickens, Rushdie, Marquez, Lawrence or any of the authors here cited as classic. None the less, as I read them, the tenor of these responses is optimistic. Reading the classics won't make you healthy or wealthy, but it probably will make you wise(r) and hopefully a better person.

Postscript – my own top ten (all twentieth-century):

1. *Ulysses* by James Joyce

2. *The End of the Affair* by Graham Greene

3. *Brideshead Revisited* by Evelyn Waugh

4. *The Bell* by Iris Murdoch

5. *Time's Arrow* by Martin Amis

6. *Possession* by A. S. Byatt

7. *A Clockwork Orange* by Anthony Burgess

8. *Beloved* by Toni Morrison

9. *Crash* by J. G. Ballard

10. *A House for Mr Biswas* by V. S. Naipaul

JOHN SUTHERLAND *is Lord Northcliffe Professor of Modern English Literature at University College, London.*

The Questions

The contributors to *The Test of Time* were sent a letter which included the following questions:

1. What is your definition of a 'classic' novel? Do you think the term 'classic' useful in connection with literature? Do you have an alternative? How did you feel about 'classics' as a schoolchild, if you felt anything at all? Was there a classic you were obliged to read at school that put you off for years (or the reverse)? Who do you feel is writing with an eye to the twenty-first century? What qualities do you think a novel will need to demonstrate to assure readership in the twenty-first century?

2. Please nominate ten essential 'classic' novels for the next 100 years. (Your selection can be from anything currently in print, or notable for being out of print, and can include titles already deemed 'classics' for whatever reason.)

3. Please nominate a maximum of ten books that you believe should never have been called 'classics'. Why have you picked on these in particular?

The Responses

Liz Attenborough

What is your definition of a classic?

Classic is now such a well-worn word that it's probably more off-putting than encouraging when used beside a book title. For me the books that matter are the ones I either think I would like to read again, or the ones I know I want to press into someone else's hands immediately. What I want most of all is a brilliantly told story that I can lose myself in completely. These, then, come under the simple title of 'favourite'. But favourites change for different times and different people. Currently Alex Garland's *The Beach* is my favourite book to recommend to older teenagers (especially boys) who think they aren't that thrilled with reading novels. But I wouldn't give it to my mother-in-law.

I don't remember being fed the idea that books were classics when I was young, as books either came into the category of school (to be studied and picked at) or home (to be chosen by me for my own pleasure). I know I picked at *Under the Greenwood Tree* in class, and didn't much like it. But somehow I found *The Woodlanders*, and wept over it and kept the final paragraph on the wall beside my bed for several years. What does that say about my young reader's view of Thomas Hardy? Probably not a lot. Now I'm sad that some books are labelled as children's classics just because they may happen to have a child somewhere near the centre. But books like *The Water Babies* or *Lorna Doone* are really not best suited to anyone at the start of their reading career, and perhaps miss out by being mislabelled.

I know I would re-read any Jane Austen, any Charles Dickens, any

D. H. Lawrence, any Evelyn Waugh at any time. So it's authors I would highlight, perhaps more than individual books. When it comes to individual books, why stick to novels? For me Virginia Axline's *Dibs: In Search of Self* is a classic work, as is Michael Holroyd's *Lytton Strachey*, and Dava Sobel's *Longitude* is stunning and will surely last. Frank McCourt's *Angela's Ashes* would be on my list of personal favourites from recent reading, and is a book I know I'll be giving to other people and will read again. In fact I find myself more likely to give people books other than novels – biography, memoir, travel writing. Is fiction too personal to share, too risky to give saying, 'I know you'll love this'?

What are your ten essential classic novels for the next 100 years?

My current fiction tips for longevity would include:

Possession by A. S. Byatt (completely involving)

What's Bred in the Bone by Robertson Davies (and any other books by him)

St Agnes's Stand by Thomas Eidson (I would never have suspected that I wanted to read about the Wild West)

One Flew over the Cuckoo's Nest by Ken Kesey (is it now the book or the film that I have in my memory?)

Cider with Rosie by Laurie Lee (what a sense of place he conjures up)

A Dance to the Music of Time sequence by Anthony Powell and *The Raj Quartet* by Paul Scott (two totally engrossing sagas that could have gone on and on)

A Suitable Boy by Vikram Seth (a book I hated to finish, and so read very slowly towards the end)

Of Mice and Men by John Steinbeck (such a powerful book, that stays with the reader for a very long time)

A Secret History by Donna Tartt (what an atmosphere)

Ask me the same question a few months from now and a host of other fondly remembered reads will come to the forefront of my mind. Isn't that the joy of being a reader – there is just so much still to discover?

LIZ ATTENBOROUGH *has had a distinguished career in publishing and is currently the Project Director for the National Year of Reading.*

J. G. Ballard

What is your definition of a classic?

We all agree about the classic novels of the past – *Robinson Crusoe, Pride and Prejudice, Great Expectations, Ulysses* – but it's surprisingly difficult to predict which contemporary novels, if any, will be the classics of the future. It ought to be easy – look for the qualities that identify the classic novel, such as a strong story and intriguing characters, a fresh and imaginative use of language, an element of vision, and a way of seeing the world that belongs uniquely to the author.

Yet too many novelists, some of them Nobel Prize-winners, who were once considered 'great' have now sunk into oblivion or are well on their way towards it – J. B. Priestley, Pearl Buck, A. J. Cronin, John O'Hara and scores of others who enjoyed large sales and respectful reviews.

It's clear that the novelists of our own day who go on to become the classics of the future will do so for reasons that aren't obvious at all. And they will face competition from a range of new media, like the Internet and the interactive CD-Rom, that will pose the sort of head-on challenge that film once faced from television.

But film survived, and I am confident that the novel will survive, in its familiar page-turning, non-interactive form. Part of the reason is the uniquely private nature of the relationship between writer and reader. No one else is involved, there are no story conferences, temperamental actors who fluff their lines, or pressure from the producer to cut back on expensive sets or too many close-ups.

What are your ten essential classic novels for the next 100 years?

I assume that most of the eighteenth- and nineteenth-century classics will still be read in a hundred years' time. If they can survive the twentieth century, with all its change and turmoil, they can survive anything. But which novels written in my own lifetime (I was born in 1930) will survive to the year 2099? Here are my guesses:

Brave New World by Aldous Huxley. This vision of the future seems uncannily accurate – test-tube babies, legalised drugs, virtual reality films, a life of compulsory pleasure. The best guide-book I know to the day after tomorrow.

Animal Farm and *Nineteen Eighty-four* by George Orwell. Some people have started to dismiss *Nineteen Eighty-four*, as if the threat of Stalinist totalitarianism has passed forever. If only that were true.

Catch-22 by Joseph Heller. War seen as a lunatic playground, a picture of the mid-twentieth century that will fascinate our descendants.

The Alexandria Quartet by Lawrence Durrell. Its lush romanticism will show how touchingly sentimental we could be.

The Loved One by Evelyn Waugh. A brilliantly mischievous glimpse of the other side of the Hollywood dream.

Lolita by Vladimir Nabokov. Wit and verbal elegance make even the darkest fantasies acceptable, or so we like to think.

The Naked Lunch by William Burroughs. A roller-coaster ride through hell that is the *Don Quixote* of the drug world.

The Big Sleep by Raymond Chandler. The purest distillation of Hollywood noir, the dark shadow cast by the Californian sun.

The Martian Chronicles by Ray Bradbury. Visionary short stories from the poet of modern science fiction.

What are the books you believe should never have been called classics?

Few contemporary novels today are called classics, but some seem to have been over-praised in a way that suggests our deep need to assign greatness to a favoured few of those around us, if only to affirm our belief in ourselves.

But will the novels of Thomas Pynchon, Philip Roth and Norman Mailer survive? Will anyone fifty years from now want to read Angus Wilson or Kingsley Amis? The three American novelists seem over-blown and self-immersed, while the British are deeply parochial, writing about matters of no interest to anyone outside our islands. All these writers are more famous than their books, a sure sign of the second-rate. But perhaps our descendants will relish Mickey Spillane and Jeffrey Archer, for reasons that none of us are now astute enough to grasp. Fiction, fortunately, thrives on uncertainty.

J. G. BALLARD *is the author of many works of fiction, including* Empire of the Sun *and* Crash. *His most recent novel,* Cocaine Nights, *was shortlisted for the Whitbread Novel Award.*

Richard Beswick

What is your definition of a classic?

One person's essential classic is inevitably another's unreadable instrument of torture, its spine (pale green if it's – as a lot of my tormentors are – an old Penguin Modern Classic) slyly eyeing you from a shelf, challenging you to go on, give me, *Nostromo*, one last go. (Conrad is in fact a strong contender for my mother-of-all *bêtes noires*, having caused my first real essay crisis when I was forced to read and precis *Lord Jim* at the age of twelve.) However, I am sure I was partly put off my old friend *Nostromo* by some tweedy pedagogue telling me, 'It's a classic, you know'. Perhaps while classics – in particular nineteenth-century ones – remain part of school syllabuses, they should be referred to as 'Great' books – as could a balanced selection of contemporary writing. There could be a sliding cinema-style 'admission scale' – 14, 16, 18 – protecting younger readers from, for example, an off-putting, premature encounter with *Emma* or a bruising early brush with *Ulysses*.

But whatever your personal prejudices, classic status must surely denote an element of proven longevity, a result of an almost Darwinian set of survival characteristics. Memorable characters and plot are a given and always will be, but to those attributes you can add what lifts a good story to a great one: an originality of tone and viewpoint that changes the way in which the reader sees the world. Books that succeed in fulfilling these criteria deserve every opportunity to survive and thrive (it's the responsibility of schools, publishers and retailers to keep promoting them to find new generations of readers) and there's no reason why the twenty-first century should be any different from the nineteenth in this respect.

What are your ten essential classic novels for the next 100 years?

The starting point for this list is that it accepts the survival qualities of *Middlemarch*, *The Woman in White*, etc. These novels are proven essentials already. What might be more interesting to see is which novels from, say, a generation ago – the last twenty-five years – will be called classics in 2099. I'd vote for all of these:

The New York Trilogy by Paul Auster. The strangest, most seductive thriller you could read.

All the Pretty Horses by Cormac McCarthy. A book that reinvents the genre of the western and mints a language of its own.

London Fields by Martin Amis. Contains the best scene ever set in a curry restaurant.

The Complete Short Stories by William Trevor. Breaking a rule for one of the few short-story writers whose short fiction is as satisfying as any full-length novel.

My Son's Story by Nadine Gordimer. Political novels are often necessarily transitory – but this, for me, is the great novel of Apartheid.

A Suitable Boy by Vikram Seth. As Tolstoy demanded of writers, it makes a world of its own.

The Unbearable Lightness of Being by Milan Kundera. Brilliant laughter-in-the-dark novel of anti-totalitarianism.

Dinner at the Homesick Restaurant by Anne Tyler. Wonderfully funny and tender novel on a small scale but with a huge emotional resonance.

Life: A User's Manual by George Perec. A huge encyclopedic masterpiece – a Chinese box of parodies, jokes and stories.

The Van by Roddy Doyle. For its sheer energy and consistent ability to make me laugh.

What are the books you believe should never have been called classics?

The Hate List:

Women in Love by D. H. Lawrence. Lawrence now seems impossibly dated and he could easily occupy spots 1–5 on this list.

Nostromo by Joseph Conrad. As they say, one of those books that demands re-reading because it's virtually impossible to remember what's happened two pages ago.

Moll Flanders by Daniel Defoe. Endless, tedious coupling.

The Lord of the Rings by J. R. R. Tolkien. A 900–page book about a load of trolls. Say no more.

For Whom the Bell Tolls by Ernest Hemingway. Novels where sex plays a big part – though pioneering in their day – often date very quickly. The earth may have moved for Hemingway's characters then but it's the reader who shudders now.

To the Lighthouse by Virginia Woolf. There is obviously a right and a wrong time for any book and attempting as a seventeen-year old to tackle Virginia Woolf's subtle essay in modernism on a topless beach in Biarritz was almost certainly a mistake.

The Ambassadors by Henry James. I love *The Portrait of a Lady, The Europeans*, etc., but the connoisseurs swear by the late James. I swear at it.

Sexus by Henry Miller. Just preposterous – see earlier comments about sex-related novels.

The House at Pooh Corner by A. A. Milne. I agree with Dorothy Parker – 'Tonstant weader fwowed up'.

Beowulf
A very, very old book but not a classic.

RICHARD BESWICK *is Editorial Director of the Abacus publishing imprint.*

Terence Blacker

What is your definition of a classic?

When I visited a school not so long ago, a teacher told me of the father of a little girl of eleven who had a simple rule so far as reading was concerned: only *bona fide* classics would be allowed in the family home. All non-classics were banned. The result, of course, was that the child was utterly uninterested in reading. And who can blame her?

I loathe the snobbery and intellectual laziness behind the idea of the classic novel. For me, a book generally regarded as a classic ceases to be a personal friend and becomes something solid, socially acceptable and morally improving. It's a school prefect, set up by my betters as a model of how to write. I want to thumb my nose at its pages.

And what exactly is a classic novel? One written to last, written carefully, written with feeling and intelligence that looks beyond and beneath the everyday surface of things, that adduces the spirit of the age? Surely any serious novel sets out to do this. To decide that some do, and become that mysterious thing 'a classic', while the rest languish pointlessly in the outer darkness is crass and simplistic.

Not that one should be surprised by the sudden concern with dividing living literature into lists. We live in a lazy, snobbish culture in which everything, from records to food to celebrities, must be graded and given marks, as if even books were now competing on some idiotic Paul Gambaccini hit parade.

So I dread to hear one of my favourite books described as 'a classic'. However much I love it, I sense that it has gone over to the other side. It is now approved majority reading, a book which plump suburbanites give each other in handtooled bindings at Christmas, that politicians pretend they read once a year, that the BBC will shortly adapt into an agreeable family drama for Sunday evenings. It has become less a novel than a social artifact, like a nice china pot or an agreeable landscape painting over the mantelpiece.

Ban classics, I say. The good, the very good and the brilliant novel is good enough for me.

What are your ten essential classic novels for the next 100 years?

I would like to include ten brilliant post-war novels (not essential, not classic, maybe not even the best, but just worth reading) that will give future generations an idea of what living in the late twentieth century was like.

Pale Fire by Vladimir Nabokov

Something Happened by Joseph Heller

The Erl-King by Michel Tournier

The Tin Drum by Gunter Grass

Money by Martin Amis

The Story of My Life by Jay McInerney

Is This Allowed? by William Donaldson

A Thousand Acres by Jane Smiley

Sabbath's Theater by Philip Roth

Rabbit at Rest by John Updike

What are the books you believe should never have been called classics?

No, I really don't like sneering at books. It's not the fault of any novel that it has been described as 'a classic' by lazy listmakers. If it has, it needs all the help it can get to be restored from the respectable to the ranks of the loved and the read.

TERENCE BLACKER *is a journalist, children's author and novelist.*

Alain de Botton

What is your definition of a classic?

The best 'classic' novels are an odd mixture. On the one hand, they tend to be written by people with strange names and are set in increasingly distant and peculiar ages, where the clothes never get dry-cleaned and the characters fight duels, go to balls, ride horses and take snuff. But they also pull off the miraculous feat of speaking to us more directly, more urgently than anything written in our own time. While seemingly engaged in her own love story in nineteenth-century rural France, Emma Bovary will continue to shed light on the romantic travails of people living in twenty-first-century space-stations.

That's the ideal scenario. Unfortunately, books rarely seem more boring than when they've been recommended to us as 'classics', perhaps because the word is synonymous with the schoolroom, tedium and the need to pass an exam. There's something terrifying about a book whose greatness we will have no choice but to accept, because generations of critics have gushed with all the authority at their disposal. How difficult to be spontaneous when reading a book we know we'll simply have to end up loving, or we'll be the only person in the world not to get *Middlemarch* or to think that perhaps *To the Lighthouse* is a bore.

I remember the relief I experienced on reading that the 'great' Dr. Johnson had no time for Laurence Sterne's 'great' novel, *Tristram Shandy*, that Stendhal had a lifelong hatred of Racine, that Flaubert had mixed feelings about Victor Hugo, that Mario Vargas

Llosa didn't like *Ulysses* and that Milan Kundera had reservations about George Orwell. There was relief here because, however obvious it might seem, it showed that there's no need to like every supposedly classic writer. One might agree with Dr. Johnson's taste (I don't), but one can trust him as a man who had his own taste, arguably a more important faculty.

As for what qualities a novel will need to demonstrate to assure readership in twenty-first century, all the same qualities that classics have ever needed, given that human beings will probably continue to be roughly the same until cloning really takes off around the twenty-second century. However, writers could help their readers by writing short books, nothing you couldn't finish on a London-Edinburgh space-shuttle flight.

What are your ten essential classic novels for the next 100 years?

Don Quixote by Cervantes

Tristram Shandy by Laurence Sterne

The Sorrows of Young Werther by Goethe

Madame Bovary by Gustave Flaubert

Anna Karenina by Leo Tolstoy

The Portrait of a Lady by Henry James

In Search of Lost Time by Marcel Proust

The Man without Qualities by Robert Musil

The Catcher in the Rye by J. D. Salinger

The Book of Laughter and Forgetting by Milan Kundera

All of them profound, and very unboring.

What are the books you believe should never have been called classics?

I've never managed to appreciate anything by Dostoevsky (my fault), nor anything by Zola (more his fault, I think).

ALAIN DE BOTTON *is the author of three novels* – Essays in Love, The Romantic Movement *and* Kiss and Tell – *and a work of non-fiction*, How Proust Can Change Your Life.

André Brink

What is your definition of a classic?

We've all become so blasé, so cynical and so suspicious, that the term 'classic novel' is more likely to be met by hoots of derision than by acclaim. Yet even if the term itself may be suspect, there's something to be said for the concept of singling out some novels as special. Because they seem to have the kind of quality which helps them outlive their age? Not necessarily because they demonstrate 'eternal values' (whatever those may be), but because they, more than others, appear to have something valid and exciting to say to successive ages or generations. *Don Quixote* would be such a one, having held its own for nearly four hundred years now – not because some group of powerful 'decision-makers' has canonised it, but because innumerable readers, in many countries, have been entertained, moved, stimulated and enriched by it. Doris Lessing once spoke amusingly about books which 'utterly and totally change your life – for at least two weeks'. But the point is that there *are* books that change one's life, one's view of the world, one's sense of belonging to the world. I know that all the really important turning points in my own life can be traced, not primarily to people I encountered (with the exception, perhaps, of Mandela), or events I was involved in, but to books. To Paton's *Cry, the Beloved Country*, to Dostoevsky's *The Idiot*, to *A Tale of Two Cities*, to *Les Misérables*, to *Kristin Lavransdatter*.

Because I grew up in small villages in the arid heart of the South African countryside, where English was quite literally a foreign language, the classics we were required to read had the fascination of the exotic, the strange, the totally-other; and so even if it often was a struggle simply to understand them, there was always the sense of grappling with something miraculous. Which meant that I never found them tedious, never revolted against them. (Though I *really* didn't like *The Pilgrim's Progress*.) Afrikaans 'classics' were different. I read them because I had to, sure, but they formed in my mind the picture of the classic novel as an unmitigated bore, dealing as they invariably did with drought, poor whites and locusts. One result was that it took me years to work through that prejudice and learn to be enthralled by *The Grapes of Wrath* or *The Story of an African Farm*.

I'm not sure I like your question, *Who do you feel is writing with an eye to the twenty-first century?* Any writer who consciously does that is prone to take himself too seriously (this type is more often than not 'he'); and that practically guarantees failure of one kind or another, whether in Solzhenitsyn or Norman Mailer or, somewhat further back, Jean-Paul Sartre. Those who have it in them to last into the next millennium are, surely, the ones who evidently enjoy what they're doing. That is, those who excel in telling *stories*. Like Scheherazade, the only writer who deserves to survive is the one who can literally defy death by the weaving of short or tall tales.

What are your ten essential classic novels for the next 100 years?

And so my ten essential 'classic' novels for the next 100 years would all belong to this category. It is very, very hard to select only ten. You did not specify whether they should all be English novels; and that makes it incomparably more difficult. But here goes:

Don Quixote de la Mancha by Miguel de Cervantes. The world in one book, crazy and funny and incomparably sad and wise, with a totality of vision matched only by Shakespeare, and down to earth and soaring in dreams, and with some of the most memorable lines in any language. 'Let us step very carefully, gentlemen, for this year there are no birds in last year's nests.'

Tristram Shandy by Laurence Sterne. The greatest fun-fair of all novels, turning any and every thought into the magic of story.

Les Misérables by Victor Hugo, for its unashamed romanticism, its mixture of the sublime and the grotesque, its redemptive grace for even the darkest recesses of the human mind.

George Eliot. I suppose I should say *Middlemarch*, but for sentimental reasons I'll take *The Mill on the Floss*, as one of the quintessential love stories of all literature, all the darker and the more moving for concerning a sister and a brother.

The Idiot by Fyodor Dostoevsky, in which the fire of a truly creative mind succeeds in fusing Don Quixote and Christ, and thereby opening up new dimensions in both – which we can recognise because in their union our own selves are subsumed.

Ulysses by James Joyce. That inimitable fanfare for the common man, in which centuries of accumulated storytelling erupt in the miraculous and exuberant celebration of a single day.

Kristin Lavransdatter by Sigrid Undset, in which the long-lost tradition of Scandinavian sagas is revived to place in relief the total life of a woman from birth to old age and death. *Femina sum, et nihil humanum alienum mihi est.*

The Trial by Franz Kafka, for breaking open the egg of the everyday to reveal inside the monstrous darkness and mystery which define our frail humanity.

One Hundred Years of Solitude by Gabriel Garcia Marquez. The consummate story of our century, rediscovered with joy and amazement, a marvel of narrative alchemy which produces from trivial reality the magic of the true philosopher's stone.

Midnight's Children by Salman Rushdie, which captures in its verve and the sweeping range of its imagination the tragedy and misunderstanding, the hope and the prophetic vision of so much of the Third World throughout the second half of our century.

And all of them, every single one of them, quite simply tells a story in which all the original power of the old Spanish formula, 'Once upon a time there was and there wasn't . . .' still smoulders, ready to erupt in each new reader's mind.

(But then, what of Defoe and Fielding, what of Diderot, what of Jane Austen and Charlotte Brontë, what of Hardy or Melville, Tolstoy or Conrad or Proust, or Mann or Lawrence or Graham Greene at their best, what of Faulkner, what of Nabokov, or the small classics of Jean Rhys, or J. M. Coetzee for that matter . . .? Hold, enough!)

What are the books you believe should never have been called classics?

Any 'classic' which is forced upon one becomes a dead weight, like Bunyan's sanctimonious verbiage which I've already referred to. Some of Dickens, I must confess, I find cloying upon re-reading, and dare I say that *Jane Eyre* has never been one of my favourites? But I would hesitate to declare 'they should never have been called classics', because I can see why others might have admired them. One person's classic is another's crap. Perhaps in the new century we may become a bit more cautious, and a bit more tolerant, towards the choices of others. What is important about making these lists, after all, is the fun of it. Individuals in the next century, like individuals in ours, will ultimately decide for themselves. One hopes.

ANDRÉ BRINK *is the author of over a dozen novels, including* A Dry White Season, Imaginings of Sand *and the recently published* Devil's Valley.

Julie Burchill

What is your definition of a classic?

I think there is something rather vulgar and depressing about the term 'classic' novel: it has become irretrievably linked with ham-fisted television serials on a Sunday night which you watch miserably before packing your satchel for school the next morning. And it does seem rather silly to lump *Ivanhoe* in with *The Catcher in the Rye*. Calling a book a classic is the quickest way to put children off them at school, as I know from bitter experience. I read everything I could get my paws on up to the age of twelve, then the hormones kicked in and I would *only* read trash in case my teachers approved of me – vile thought. I think Lorrie Moore and Shena Mackay will last into the next century, but I don't think many of the self-adoring Big Boys will. Nothing dates faster than This Year's Model.

What are your ten essential classic novels for the next 100 years?

Hangover Square by Patrick Hamilton – most beautiful novel ever written.

Redhill Rococo by Shena Mackay – like a box of chocolates with no boring nuts.

Anagrams by Lorrie Moore – all the shimmering sorrow of being a young American.

Namedropper by Emma Forrest – *The Catcher in the Rye* for the Tamagochi generation.

The Diary of a Nobody by George and Weedon Grossmith – most comforting novel ever written.

Brighton Rock by Graham Greene – overwrought but majestic.

Tourist by Matt Thorne – as sad as Sunday and as sexy as a scar.

As Good as it Gets by Simon Nolan – funniest novel ever about the pleasures and pitfalls of drug-taking.

Cold Comfort Farm by Stella Gibbons – funniest book ever written.

Ambition by Julie Burchill – best novel about the Eighties ever written.

What are the books you believe should never have been called classics?

Animal Farm by George Orwell – simplistic tosh.

Nineteen Eighty-four by George Orwell – ditto. You can tell he's an old Etonian. Commie-baiting at a level the *Sun* would find unacceptable.

On the Road by Jack Kerouac – stoned fag too doped to get out of the closet.

Sons and Lovers by D. H. Lawrence – perspiring pervert gets it wrong again.

Cider with Rosie by Laurie Lee – bred a generation of schoolchildren who couldn't look at a book without wanting to burn it.

The Great Gatsby by F. Scott Fitzgerald – self-adoring swill.

As well as being a journalist, JULIE BURCHILL *is the author of several works of non-fiction and a novel,* Ambition.

Gordon Burn

What is your definition of a classic?

'As unlettered as a porch monkey.' This is a phrase that has stayed
with me from an essay Richard Ford once wrote about the writers –
Hemingway, Faulkner, Fitzgerald – who brought him to literature.
Who taught him that book reading could be a pleasure, that is to
say, rather than an imposition and a chore. I have remembered it
because I felt I *was* it – somebody with gaps in his readings of the
'classics' as wide and windswept as the Sahara and quite happy to
accept that this was just the way things were.

I was at school at a time – the 1960's – and in a place – Newcastle
– when considerable art in any area was hard-pressed to compete
with the almost weekly mini-masterpieces from the likes of Roy
Orbison and Dionne Warwick and the Searchers and all the other
excitements in the air. Newcastle was the home of the Club A Go-Go
and the Animals and also the Mordern Tower where Tom and
Connie Pickard organised readings by Allen Ginsberg and Gary
Snyder and Basil Bunting and Stevie Smith and Robert Creeley.
There were books on sale there by Gurdjieff, Ouspensky, Reich,
Burroughs, Genet. People got pissed; passed out; smoked dope. And
back at school the next day you were expected to plough through
Austen and Defoe and *A Pattern of Islands*.

The irony was that I was bookish by nature. A booksniff. I like
books. I devoured them. But only when there was a sense of
discovery involved; of feasting rather than being force-fed. There
was always something churchy about 'the classics', and especially

then. They always seemed to be bonnet books, even if they had only
been written a few decades earlier. Probably it was a class thing –
that divide between pupils and teachers, if not necessarily between
writers and readers. Popular culture to that time had been more
constrained, because there was another culture which had been
more dominant. There was a gap – a roaring gulf – between the life
being lived and life as it was represented in novels. The writers we
were given to read weren't like us. What they wrote about didn't
remind us of ourselves or sanction our lives. In many ways this was
inevitable. We were only the second generation of teenagers,
making it new, inventing as we went. Pop culture (as opposed to
the popular culture of the pre-war years) hadn't been written about
in a significant way – hadn't been made the subject of plays and
operas and novels – because it was still in the process of being
invented. But even that would have been news to the English and
Latin masters at my grammar school in Newcastle. To them, difficult
art was the only art that could light up a life; still the only area worth
considering.

I remember one morning at the end of the 1960's poking my
long hair in the back of my collar, putting on a tie and taking a bus
out to the secondary-modern at Whitley Bay where I was due to start
as an English teacher at the beginning of the winter term. It was
Christmas-party time and there was music and dancing and running
in the corridors, which of course wasn't permitted. I was dismayed to
learn that the head of the department for whom I would be working
hadn't heard of Ken Loach's film, *Kes*, which had been released
several months earlier, or the Barry Hines novel from which it had
been adapted. That night I went to see The Who at the Mayfair
Ballroom. The next morning I parcelled up the grammars and
primers and the timetable I had been given and sent them back to
the people I had got them from with a note saying sorry, but no
thanks.

It took a decade or so for the novel to catch up with the work that
Norman Mailer, Truman Capote, Tom Wolfe and others had been
doing in the area of non-fiction. And it seems to me that not

necessarily the best (what is that?), but the defining writing of this American century will be the writing to be found on the borderline between real and invented life (the true-life-novel, as practised by Mailer and Naipaul; autobiography-as-fiction) and at the collision sites of standard and vernacular English – writing that feeds on the jargons of showbiz and blag and tabloid surreality and bare-faced hucksterism. The language of the mediated transactions and synthetic pleasures that have become the condition of city living in this last part of the twentieth century. Bellow, Tom Wolfe, Martin Amis and Don DeLillo were among the first to see the poetry in the junk, the first to recognise and harness the energies of low-living and ad-speak and common vulgarity and sleaze. They saw the potential of using language for and of itself, extemporising around it, riffing on it, *inventing* it, in the process ditching the novel's traditional virtues of characterisation, narrative tension, psychological complexity and the rest. They speak for the times. They lost the plot.

What are your ten essential classic novels for the next 100 years?

My ten modern classics, in no particular order, are:

The Enigma of Arrival by V. S. Naipaul

A House for Mr Biswas by V. S. Naipaul

The Great Gatsby by F. Scott Fitzgerald

The Executioner's Song by Norman Mailer

White Noise by Don DeLillo

Oh What A Paradise it Seems by John Cheever

The Right Stuff by Tom Wolfe (as much a novel as *The Executioner's Song* or *In Cold Blood*, as well as his own later novels, as far as I'm concerned)

The Sportswriter by Richard Ford

Sons and Lovers by D. H. Lawrence

Radcliffe by David Storey

What are the books you believe should never have been called classics?

I have no comment on the most over-rated – I haven't read enough of them to form an opinion, although it no longer feels something to be proud of.

GORDON BURN *is the author of two novels* – Alma Cogan *and* Fullalove *– and several works of non-fiction, including* Happy Like Murderers.

John Calder

What are your ten essential classic novels for the next 100 years?

I am not just a publisher and author, but a reader of about 100 or more books a year, so to make a choice of ten classics is not easy. I have picked ten very different books, all written in the twentieth century, but others keep intruding on my memory. I have had to leave out Thomas Mann, Rosamund Lehmann, Iris Murdoch, Doris Lessing, Camus, Sartre, Gide, Robbe-Grillet, Koestler, all of whom have played a part in the literature of the twentieth century. Of the ten, there are some I have known and published, but I do not think my assessment is influenced by that. Here are the ten:

Remembrance of Things Past by Marcel Proust. I give the English title. This many-volumed novel is not only a panoramic vision of French life on the higher social level, bringing a whole vanishing world into focus, but it was the cause of that world vanishing. After being so graphically described so that it could recognise itself in all its artificiality, it had to change. The same thing happened to pre-Revolutionary France because of the similar plays of Beaumarchais. But it is also a great philosophical novel that tells the reader how to live and how to increase our life span by keeping past memory always in the present, and how to die stoically and poetically. Proust shows time as elastic, constantly enriching the present with the past.

Ulysses by James Joyce. Proust brought a society to life, Joyce a city. In doing so he also gave new possibilities to language by transforming it into the language of the mind. The mind does not work chronologically like classical literature but is full of private fantasies, recollections, associations, elastic, as Proust demonstrated. By portraying the collective mind of a whole city and especially the thoughts, conversations and obsessions of his selected characters, Joyce gave us a new view of multi-layered humanity, but at the same time demonstrated how language works or can work in the hands of an experimental genius. He also makes the reader work harder, which is a way of increasing his intelligence and perception as well as his (or her) knowledge.

The Castle by Franz Kafka. Kafka makes us recognise what we all feel, but do not often want to recognise – our total unimportance in the great scheme of things, whatever that is. We are all small, frightened people in an immense and terrifying world that we cannot comprehend. We all live in a state of menace and uncertainty. He was also prescient in recognising, as a Jew in the German community of Prague, the Nazi menace that was about to descend on Europe and he instinctively recognised in the German historical character those traits that would make the Holocaust possible. He was a humble man and the perfect antidote to those who feel or are encouraged in the age of hype to think of themselves as being in some way important.

The Molloy Trilogy by Samuel Beckett. The three above-named writers all changed the way we view the world and language. Beckett is the summation of the three, showing humanity, with great compassion and much wit to relieve the bleakness of his message, as it really is, but choosing to do so by portraying the drop-outs of society. He portrays man as having an inventive and observant mind in a body that starts decaying at birth, and the mind-body relationship is central to his large body of work. Life is unavoidable tragedy, but we can relieve our own suffering by helping others and not returning the cruelty we suffer from others or a malign destiny to those worse off than ourselves. His message is ethical: be kind. But he writes in both prose and poetry with a force unequalled since Shakespeare, and with a magnificent use of language, sparer in the later work, that is paradoxically a joy and an inspiration to the reader. He may be seen as the greatest literary figure of the century.

To the Lighthouse by Virginia Woolf. Virginia Woolf follows on in the social novelistic tradition that runs from Jane Austen to Galsworthy, but in capturing the Edwardian era she shows an idyllistic upper-middle-class world about to be devastated by the First World War that destroyed that class and its values. Under the gentleness of everyday security lies a feeling for destiny about to take its toll. Her prose is more complex than her predecessors' because it reflects a thinking mind that does not take surface reality for granted. Lost hopes and aspirations, missed opportunities, unhappiness resolutely damped down because it is un-English, and a refusal to broaden that English horizon with deeper culture: that is the essence of the gentle satire of Woolf, but regret and nostalgia are also there.

The Grapes of Wrath by John Steinbeck. Of the social realistic writers of the American Thirties, Steinbeck has lasted longest, perhaps because this novel in particular has been successfully filmed and dramatised. It is a biting indictment of what capitalism does to the dreams of the ordinary man and of the stupidity of that same man who does not understand what he is doing and how to look to the future. One of the best pictures of its time, with a deep anger running under the story.

Tropic of Cancer by Henry Miller. Miller is a true writer and only intermittently a good one, but the honesty, which depends on self-satire, was new in its day and has inspired many others to come out from behind their cloaks and masks and say what they really think. He opened the flood-gates of sexuality to literary exploration, not to exploit, but to explore. He was a pioneer.

Animal Farm by George Orwell. No book is more detested in those regimes that preach socialism, equality and universal well-being but practise tyranny, corruption and a new class system, than this clever and biting satire. It applies wherever power is concentrated in only a few hands. It is the masterpiece of a truly democratic mind of great integrity and independence.

The Naked Lunch by William Burroughs. A horrifying picture of modern humanity by a writer whose mind is in his bowels, recalling the world of Bosch. Burroughs is in the Expressionist tradition, using dreams, fantasy and experiment in a way that recalls painterly techniques more than literary ones. He is an icon in the world of drug culture, although he points out all its dangers. A book about which normal definitions relating to quality or style do not apply. It is what it is, and is important to modern literature because of its obsessive contents.

The Georgics by Claude Simon. The masterpiece (but not the only one) of a Nobel Prize-winning writer who is difficult to read because of his self-indulgence in filling his first hundred pages with diffuse and unnecessary descriptive matter. His subject is war and what it does both to civilians and combatants. Simon is brilliant in capturing the atmosphere of war, the panic and horror, and he writes from personal experience. The waste, the lost dreams, the destruction, and the reasons why it happens, all are here.

JOHN CALDER *is the managing director of independent publisher Calder Publications.*

Frank Delaney

What is your definition of a classic?

The classic 'novel' must first answer to the classic definition: 'A fictitious prose narrative or tale of considerable length (now usually long enough to fill one or more volumes), in which characters and actions representative of the real life of past or present times are portrayed in a plot of more or less complexity.' That's the OED.

Think, too, of Dr Johnson's definition: 'A small tale, generally of love.' Or of a paraphrased definition which would sum up as, 'A work of prose invention reflecting the human condition.'

As for the term 'classic', we use it for an FM radio station, cars that shudder to and from Brighton once a year, ageing Hollywood beauties and the movies they starred in, or cheese, wine, knitwear. Meaning something timelessly appealing and retaining all and more of the qualities first admired in it.

We aspire to it. 'Classic' is a term meaning both quality and vibrant appeal. I should like to be thought of as a classic anything – kisser, rose-grower, adventurer (but never, forfend, a classic bore). So a classic novel is one which tells us about the world old or new in a way that will last forever and evergreen. Useless things definitions, except to lexicographers. If we are to have 'classic' in association with literature, better choose by example.

Here we find two categories: those we are, or were, constantly told to think of as classics. Fielding's *Tom Jones* – but you have to skip-read in order not to lose the plot or your concentration; *The Pilgrim's Progress*, which, you will have been assured, will make you feel virtuous (not when you're fourteen-years old it won't, whatever its beauty). *Tristram Shandy* bothers many but I love it; *The Vicar of Wakefield* suffers a cordial hatred in my family, but again not from me – or is it Goldsmith I love? And I am weary of Walpole and the other Gothics – but never tire of Melville.

This might suggest that I am not good at judging 'classic' material – because the term 'classic' seems to presuppose that we will like it whether we like it or not, and it will be good for us whether we feel that good reaching us. Luckily, all subjective matter is wide enough for us to find things we actually can like, and be pleased to like, while still belonging in the church, so to speak.

The list is not endless but it is long. I will join in with all of Jane Austen's supporters, all of Dickens's, and all of James Joyce's, and I do so without hesitation. A slight, inquiring 'Hm?' will accompany any unfettered Brontë-ism and certain Hardy annuals. I will hope for support in my campaign for George Eliot and, a little less warmly, Thackeray. And I want, I emphatically insist upon, Robert Louis Stevenson, D. H. Lawrence and E. M. Forster. Conrad, Henry James and Hemingway. Two more: *Madame Bovary* and *The Great Gatsby* rise in some ways above all others, leaving Flaubert and Scott Fitzgerald bringing up a substantial rear (as they often did, I expect, in their turbulent lives).

But this is no rump parliament. This list marries the term 'classic' as I know it, understand it and was taught it to passionate personal liking, and thereupon I dance upon the ground as mapped. This, for me, moves closer to the definition of 'classic' in literature than any list of the 'Ten Best Ever' can hope to do. 'Classic' means a novel of which we have formed a never-changing opinion which combines feelings of love for its flesh-and-blood and being moved by its greatness; when I pick it up I want to read it now no matter how often I have already done so.

Now lists stretch to the horizon: *Anna Karenina*, *Crime and Punishment*, *War and Peace*, *The Moonstone*, *The Age of Innocence*, Thomas Wolfe's *Look Homeward Angel*, *To the Lighthouse*, *Nineteen Eighty-four*, William Golding's *The Spire*, Anthony Burgess's *Earthly*

Powers; Kingsley Amis's *Lucky Jim*; *Alice in Wonderland*; *The Wind in the Willows*; John Braine, Patrick White, Barbara Pym. But soon a desire takes over to stop making lists and start re-reading the books.

The blood leaps again when thinking ahead to the living authors who will reach the 'classic' lists in the Waterstone's Book Derby at Epsom Downs in 2098. Will Salman Rushdie be there? Undoubtedly – with *Midnight's Children*. So will Saul Bellow and Philip Roth and John Updike and Doris Lessing and Mordecai Richler and Martin Amis and Nadine Gordimer and Iris Murdoch and perhaps John Fowles. Richard Adams might be there with *Watership Down*. So might Frederick Forsyth with *The Day of the Jackal* – 'classic' is also a matter of genre.

Tom Wolfe? Too soon to say for something so big. Toni Morrison? Other juries have doubtless already decided – and on Maya Angelou, Germaine Greer *et al* and *inter alia*, 'classic' is also subject to political attitude and this raises the major point of any exercise such as this 'classic novel' search.

We must fear for what we now call the classic novel. The 'Dead White European Males' being exterminated daily in the curricula of American universities are a great loss to all human kind that passes through such doors – because ultimately 'classic' means only one thing: a work of art that exalts the condition and spirit of those humans who consume it, and which is therefore above all creed and posture, temporary or permanent.

Future Perfect? Nothing's perfect, it never can be – that's one of the essential thrills of writing; you can never get it right. But it is a glorious thing to have the power of future judgment. Provided we use it responsibly, provided we use it with respect for what warms our hearts and lifts our souls.

That is why the American version of political correctness – the banning of Shakespeare and Keats and Wordsworth on the ground of their not being either female or American – feels so worrying.

Conversely (even allowing for its commercial imperatives, viz., to get us to buy more books), that is also the value of this Waterstone's exercise. It will remind us of the term 'classic', reinforce the reputations of those to whom Time has justly given reputations and continue defining 'classic' and above all 'novel'. Even if sometimes it may only be 'a small tale, generally of love'.

FRANK DELANEY *is a prolific writer, journalist, broadcaster and novelist.*

Philip Dodd

What is your definition of a classic?

I've always loved novels that are huge baggy monsters – Henry
James's phrase for swollen Victorian novels, exactly what he didn't
want his own control-freak fiction novels to be. In the end aren't all
the great novels monsters, in one way or another? And not only, or
even always, in length? Like the monster in Mary Shelley's
Frankenstein, the great novels are stitched together out of bits and
pieces of carcasses. They are a hymn to our mongrel selves, to
misquote Salman Rushdie. Think of *Moby Dick*, a monstrous soup of
whaling manual, puritan tract and sea story; or Dickens's *Bleak
House*, which ends up out-Kafkaing Kafka but begins like some
freshly filed newspaper article: 'London: Michaelmas Term lately
over, and the Lord Chancellor sitting in Lincoln's Inn hall.
Implacable November weather.'

Such novels are irreplaceable. But classics? Doesn't 'classic novel'
feel a contradiction in terms? Classic equals authority, touchstone,
of the first or highest order, pertaining to the Greeks or Romans.
Novel equals new, unknown, strange. Novel is the johnny-come-
lately of literature. Born less than three hundred years ago, of
dubious parentage, it was often shunned by the literati of the time;
probably a sign of dumbing down, if only the phrase had been
available. Even as late as the 1860's, Matthew Arnold managed to
avoid mentioning a novel while mounting a defence of literature,
and went banging on instead about poetry at a moment when great
poetry could be found in Emily Brontë's novels, not her verse.

Monsters are not very keen on respectability – so be sceptical of those novels that presently crave it. Almost all of those nice literary Faber novels are not going to see the twenty-first century; but a lot of prose may. James Baldwin's essays are fine literature in a way his novels aren't. And the same is true of Angela Carter. The novels that will survive are those forged by writers still wrestling with vulgarity, uninterested in refinement. There's the wonderful (and late) Leonardo Sciascia, revelling in pretend detective novels; Kurt Vonnegut, bathing in the cheap glory of pulp fiction; and Salman Rushdie, trying to write a history of modern India and having to break most of the rules of the English novel, that epicentre of sensitivity, to do so.

Brought up like a modern American in a mining village in Yorkshire, my heroes were Eddie Cochran and John Wayne, Sonny Boy Williamson and Billie Holliday. I didn't read any classic novels, either at home or school, until my teens. That was when we moved to a city and I found my way to my local public library where literature was a solace. I made up my own pantheon, as I bumped into things – *Molloy* and *War and Peace* were favourites. Classics for me they weren't. Books for life they have turned out to be.

What are your ten essential classic novels for the next 100 years?

Novels are less a kind of literature than a world. It would be possible to list ten classic gothic novels, from *Frankenstein* to Ballard's *The Drowned World*; or ten great first-person novels, from Twain's *Huckleberry Finn* to Beckett's *The Unnameable*. But if we have to play the game, then here are the novels that are more restorative than breakfast; the ten books I would want to learn by heart, if all novels were threatened with destruction and only memory could sustain them:

Jonathan Swift's *Gulliver's Travels*, because savage comedy is more serious than tragedy; because every generation needs to drink at the cup of such unblinking acerbity.

James Hogg's *Private Memoirs and Confessions of a Justified Sinner*, because it is terrifying; because it stops the mind from being too narrow; because two fine novels, *Dr Jekyll and Mr Hyde* and Spark's *The Prime of Miss Jean Brodie* would have been still-born without it; because it may not count as a novel, which is one of the characteristics of all great novels.

Mary Shelley's *Frankenstein*, because it gave birth to one of the few modern myths; because it has the greatest chase in fiction; because it transmutes terror into tenderness.

Herman Melville's *Moby Dick*, because it is the most exhilarating and exhausting book there ever was; because it may well not be a novel; because from chapter to chapter it moves with the carelessness of all great art; because it is the most profound meditation on whiteness there is; because it has a marvellous opening; and because I would have retired if I had only written the scene where Quinque and Ishmael sleep in the same bed.

Dickens's *Little Dorrit*, because it is the London novel, where the streets and buildings have more life than the throttled characters.

Balzac's *Lost Illusions*, because it is a book for adults.

Tolstoy's *War and Peace*, because its grasp nearly matches its extraordinary ambition: to write the public and private history of a nation.

Twain's *Huckleberry Finn*, because it is so funny; because only at its end do you know what its gusto has hidden.

Joyce's *Ulysses*, because of all the modernist works it is the only one that says unmisgivingly, Yes.

Ivo Andric's *The Bridge over the Drina*, because it has more stories than any other novel I know; because it imagines matters I did not understand; because I now understand what torture can do.

What are the books you believe should never have been called classics?

Every week, some modest, newly published novel is announced by someone as a classic. But let's not waste time over reviewers or Booker Prize judges. Non-classics, in no particular order:

J. D. Salinger's *The Catcher in the Rye*, because soured romanticism palls fast.

Walter Scott's *Ivanhoe*, because I'd hate to think that the Prime Minister's praise for the novel led people to think that it was the best of Scott, when it is probably the worst.

Anything by Trollope, the novelist as comfort blanket.

Pat Barker's *Union Street*, which peddles refined disgust as insight.

Novels by George Orwell – he mislaid his genius in his non-fiction.

PHILIP DODD *is Director of the ICA.*

Sarah Dunant

What is your definition of a classic?

What is a classic novel? A book that changes your life.

I read my first 'classic' when I was 13. *Angelique* was a romantic adventure about a seventeenth-century French heroine, written by a husband-and-wife team, Sergeanne Golon. Of course you've never heard of it. And if you'd read it or any of the five others written in the series you'd probably be shocked to find me calling it a classic (though not as shocked as my mother who, when she discovered the third book, in which the lovely Angelique is raped, burst into tears and confiscated them all). But I stand my ground, because for me *Angelique* fulfilled one of the key ingredients of a classic novel – it changed my life. This compulsive story of a beautiful convent girl who marries into the aristocracy, becomes the mistress of the Sun King, falls into destitution in the Paris underworld and gets deported to the New World, gripped me to such a degree that while I was reading it I became Angelique. Seventeenth-century France was more real to me than 1960's Shepherds Bush. Through her adventures I rehearsed every major adult feeling: love, sex, grief, betrayal, pain, courage, fear. *Angelique* taught me more about life than anything in the preceding twelve years had done. It also taught me the power of narrative. When I finished the last book I was so distraught I re-read them all again, and then went ranging round the library shelves, desperate for something to fill the void. Around this time some wise adult (was it my mother thinking strategically?) threw me *Tess of the D'Urbervilles* and its mix of savage fate and history captivated me immediately. By the time I was fourteen I had read every Thomas Hardy in the library and had signed up for History O-level.

So would I put *Angelique* in my top ten classics now? Conscious of the chill winds of literary disapproval, probably not. But would I give it to my twelve-year old? You betcha. Though I'd keep *Tess of the D'Urbervilles* in reserve.

What are your ten essential classic novels for the next 100 years?

Classics I agree with:

Tess of the D'Urbervilles by Thomas Hardy

Jane Eyre by Charlotte Brontë

The Raj Quartet by Paul Scott (four books but they have to be read as one)

The Red and the Black by Stendhal

The Trial by Franz Kafka

The Name of the Rose by Umberto Eco

The Magic Toyshop by Angela Carter

See Under: Love by David Grossman

The Golden Notebook by Doris Lessing

The English Patient by Michael Ondaatje

What are the books you believe should never have been called classics?

Classics I don't agree with:

Ulysses by James Joyce. Intellectually and historically I completely understand why this novel is a classic – the problem is every time I try to read it I can't get through it. Sorry.

The Old Man and the Sea by Ernest Hemingway. Yes, yes, I know it's important for women to understand men's stuff, but this is just too elemental (or do I mean sentimental?) for me.

Far Away and Long Ago by W. H. Hudson. It's probably already fallen off the list, but good riddance. I read it ten times for O-level English and it got more boring with each reading. I vowed I'd take revenge on it then. It's taken me this long to get my wish.

The Little Prince by (I still can't remember his name). Children's classic. I didn't get this when I was young and I still don't get it now. While others find it delicate, profound and charming, I find it whimsical, fake and corny.

SARAH DUNANT *is a former presenter on* The Late Show *and the author of seven novels, including the crime novels* Fatlands *and* Transgressions.

Vanessa Feltz

What is your definition of a classic?

I loathe the term 'classic'. It seems such a specious, unhelpful and ultimately corruptible label. It can be understood to mean too many disparate, sometimes desperate things, from 'quintessentially of its time' to 'a paradigm of its ilk' and on through 'a bastion against immortality' to 'perfectly formed after the classical model'. None of these definitions appeal to me in the least. Who bestows such a title and why? At school, The Haberdashers' Aske's School for Girls, a classic felt very much like a *cabbage* – deeply dreary but, somehow, extra good for you. One would do almost anything – lacrosse, Greek O-level – to avoid being lumbered with a classic. Some utterly charming books were thoroughly ruined for me in advance by being tagged in this way – *Cider with Rosie*, for example, which I adored, but only after I realised it was nothing like Thor Heyerdahl's excruciating The *Kon-Tiki Expedition*, also hailed, Lord knows why, as a classic. Trollope's *Barchester Towers* filled me, entirely needlessly, with dread. I feared that such a classic would be unbearable. In fact, I loved it so much I still know chunks by heart. The legacy of loathing still lingers in my soul. Why else would I still have failed to read *Wuthering Heights*?

I have no way of knowing whether writers are purposely focused beyond the millennium, but I suspect that Saul Bellow, Philip Roth, A. S. Byatt, Julian Barnes and Iris Murdoch will survive long beyond it. I hope that the spawning of hi-tech alternatives will not have infected, in any way, the vital ingredients necessary to assure a novel's readership. E. M. Forster's *Aspects of the Novel* (itself, though I hate to say it, a classic) is still a useful barometer. So is *Alice's Adventures in Wonderland*. 'And what is the use of a book,' thought Alice, 'without pictures or conversations?'

What are your ten essential classic novels for the next 100 years?

I hate the idea of defaming these books by labelling them classics, but, since you ask:

Portnoy's Complaint by Philip Roth

Mrs Dalloway by Virginia Woolf

David Copperfield by Charles Dickens

Gentlemen Prefer Blondes by Anita Loos

The Van by Roddy Doyle

The Prince of West End Avenue by Alan Isler

The Great Gatsby by F. Scott Fitzgerald

Evelina by Fanny Burney

Daniel Deronda by George Eliot

Cranford by Mrs Gaskell

What are the books you believe should never have been called classics?

The Mayor of Casterbridge by Thomas Hardy – an infernal bore, a surfeit of nature and an all-round wretched read.

The Waves by Virginia Woolf – atypical Woolf, gone completely adrift.

Watership Down by Richard Adams – I prefer Walt Disney.

Mansfield Park by Jane Austen – anaemic heroine afflicted by headaches, lumpen milquetoast hero and ugly Bertram sisters who outshine Fanny's soppy Cinderella.

The Golden Bowl by Henry James – were ever sentences so laboriously entangled? Were ever characters so tediously unentangled?

VANESSA FELTZ *is a television presenter, columnist and journalist.*

Janice Galloway

What is your definition of a classic?

I've never been cozy with the word classic. Classics can become
canons and canons are often dangerously loaded. They can be
conscripted by dubious sorts for dubious reasons, be used to silence
and threaten, need careful handling blah blah blah. Even so, there's
a usefulness in shorthand, and in a world where publisher blurbs are
increasingly (morbidly, even chronically) hysterical, a word that
suggests a more measured, time-tested recommendation has to have
something going for it. Shorthand, mind. That's all. Neither of my
schools – ie Jack's Road Primary and rugby-playing Ardrossan
Academy, which belted little boys for playing football and which
never quite got used to being forced to go comprehensive –
perceived much use for the word, either, though they were certainly
taught. I recall A. A. Milne from the former, while the latter served
up at least ten Shakespeares, a straggle of Keats and Donne, four or
five stray Wordsworths, a large bouquet of Burns (Ayrshire school),
some Borders Ballads and a rash of 'moderns' – Pinter, Yeats, Dylan
Thomas, Eliot, Auden. Only the Welshman got on my nerves; the
rest I loved. *Loved.* Memorised in great swathes without trying. Some
of it brought me out in bumps. Literally. All those teenage
hormones. All poetry, plays. It seems I felt less passion for prose.
Some short stories (by Scott, Stevenson, Grassic Gibbon, Joyce)
spring to mind, an essay by Swift, but no novels. For different
reasons, no women. None at all. Till Sixth year, and a revolution of
sorts, when my music teacher gave me a thin paperback with a

woman's name on the spine. *The Prime of Miss Jean Brodie.* I read it twice. Shortly after, I found Stevie Smith and Sylvia Plath, their faces incongruous inside the classic poetry anthology where they'd been all this time, untaught. I taught them to myself, read the music teacher's next gift, a biography of Paul Robeson. Then *Bairnsangs, Wuthering Heights,* a whole cache of Jacobean erotic madrigals. Via a straight line from Chopin, Mme Sand. I flunked Maths to read opera libretti, Goethe and Schiller as lieder, Vaughan Williams' fold songs. Dickinson and Dickens, Wilde, Ionesco, Chekhov. Mrs Browning, e e cummings, The Chalet School, Orton. Good God, Hardy, Gunn, Lady Nairn. I flunked everything except Music and just read. No going back.

I cried a lot at university because my music teacher wasn't there. They offered their classics, their way, with little encouragement to lift and lay, experiment, play. By and large, too, the no-woman zone had returned. And a new thing. No Scots. Maybe I wouldn't have known any different if I'd rolled up at the gates a year earlier, but now I did. Disappointment brought me out in a terrible fit of the studies that got worse till I stopped reading altogether, left, and didn't read again for at least a couple of years. Thereafter, I read all of Hans Christian Andersen, all of *Alice*, taking care with the words as though they might explode. Learning how to do it over again. Then I bumped into Alasdair Gray's *Lanark*. And that was the beginning again. Sorted.

Classics at school taught me that what's offered matters a good deal to young people's sense of possibility. At university, I found that how it's offered matters too. In the former, I felt opened up, gifted – i.e. 'This great thing is my great thing if I want it, therefore all great things are open to me.' In the latter, I was part of the factory line – i.e. 'I'm stupid and need to be told how to understand before I'm fit to read anything for myself.' Misrepresented as ways to pass exams, trophies to tuck beneath a literary belt, as test, puzzles, or challenges to suss out people who are not like us, classics are reduced to instruments of torture or fear, and fear opens onto nothing. What my music teacher gave me – and what the uni almost drove out – was a sense of fearlessness and he was a godsend. He was also a head of department with lots of free time, a decent budget, and a maximum class-size of five – encountering him at that stage of both our careers was one of the best breaks I ever had. Five years after I hid in his rooms reading all day, I was a teacher myself. My class-sizes were on average 33!

I taught books that some of the kids had read in Primary Five (because the store-cupboard was too bankrupt to allow otherwise), taught books round the class, a chapter at a time (because the class was too big to manage any other way) and didn't single out kids to offer as much as I'd have liked to (because it would have chewed up the syllabus too fast, dumped me with marking there was no time to mark, and I'd have exploded dealing with the work-load in a matter of months) and I felt badly about it all. At the same time, Ken was leaving classroom teaching in his forties because he couldn't do the job the way he wanted any more. Some years later I did too. Neither of us felt we had much option. Most teachers, I guess, still don't. I admire teachers hugely, but the lack of morale in the profession is undeniable, the feeling of having lost the plot likewise. How children are offered possibility and books these days I have little idea. What people will read in future, whether they will read, what they will feel is open to them, accessible, theirs for the taking, is something about which I can't begin to conjecture.

What are your ten essential classic novels for the next 100 years?

Meantime, there's this. Choosing ten personally-styled classics is a nuts-driving activity. Raddled with qualifications and embarrassment, making it clear there's no such thing as essential reading, this is what I finally chose:

The Lover by Marguerite Duras, because it's spacious and terse at the same time, erotic and moving with no trace of sentimentality, explores the past and reaches into how it forms the present, suggests a future, all in just over 100 pages. Her handling of chronology is superb – very complex shifts rendered apparently effortlessly. Duras doesn't waste words or energy, and conveys more emotional truth for it.

The Last Man by Mary Shelley, because it's got as much horror and pathos as *Frankenstein,* though manages somehow to be more delicate and approachable. It contains none of the sore-thumb revisions that her husband, Percy Bysshe, smeared through *Frankenstein* in the belief he was 'sophisticating' its language: the phrasing is more direct and all Mary's. In *Frankenstein,* the monster lost a mother/father and a sense of love. In *The Last Man,* everyone does. It's terrifying.

The White Bird Passes by Jessie Kesson, because it's simple, rule-breaking, distinctly female and freeing. It's the story of the daughter of an Aberdeenshire prostitute in the early part of this century, and something I hoped would get read more following what the papers called an upsurge of interest in Scottish Literature. And it hasn't yet.

The Tenant of Wildfell Hall by Anne Brontë, because it's not like anything else, and her sisters tried to put her off publishing it, and it was taboo stuff. Its subject matters are still rare in fiction, a whole area still to be dealt with well.

The Expedition of Humphry Clinker by Tobias Smollett, because it makes me laugh out loud and because it's satire with unexpectedly tender bits, full of freshness and naivety, and its laddism is less tedious than the current kind.

Epitaph of a Small Winner by Machado de Assis, because it's genuinely original, full of anger and irony and fun and pathos and so formally risky it's hard to credit as a nineteenth-century work.

Mrs Dalloway by Virginia Woolf, because it's a huge risk of a book that must have been a bastard to write and works against all the odds. Huge emotional dramas are played against the motions of the apparently everyday, almost unconsciously. I get very angry when people come over Literary Macho about this book – 'it can't be "real" if there's no prostitutes/drugs/people being blown up in it when people are having a dinner party for godsake' – the *Loaded* school of analysis. Yes it can. It is.

Lanark by Alasdair Gray, because they're short stories that are honest, inventive, visionary, sad, funny and wise. And they Changed My Life.

The Heart is a Lonely Hunter by Carson McCullers, because it's transformative – so-called ordinariness and so-called small lives given their full quota of human striving and dignity.

Germinal by Emile Zola, because it's still shocking. Solid as boots. He writes like he's taking a photograph, everything still and keen and vivid. Another day I'd choose *Madame Bovary* for the last one. Or *Crime and Punishment. The Private Memoirs and Confessions of a Justified Sinner.* Or *North and South.* Or *The Prime of Miss Jean Brodie,* certainly *Jean Brodie. The Snow Queen.* Galt's *Annals of the Parish,* maybe. Let's face it, another day, the whole list would be different.

What are the books you believe should never have been called classics?

Finally, ten shouldn't-be classics? Dear me. I wouldn't dream of burdening people who weren't good friends with those prejudices. I will, however, go on record as saying I'd rather give President Clinton a blow-job than read *Lolita, Lady Chatterley's Lover, La Nausée* or *The Well of Loneliness* again. The whole set, mind, or no deal.

JANICE GALLOWAY *is a novelist, short-story writer and playwright.*

Martyn Goff

What is your definition of a classic?

As a child I grew up in a large house in Hampstead which had a morning room/library. There were sets of books in glass-fronted bookcases. If ever I was caught looking at them, I was reprimanded. So I waited my chance, pulled out *David Copperfield*, slipped the books along with some cardboard at the end, and made off with my trophy. I was so excited with the result that gradually over the next two years I stole, read and returned all the Dickens; all the Walter Scotts, Jane Austens, George Eliots and so on, including Dostoevsky. My definition of a classic is one of those untouchable, unread books in sets behind glass doors.

I was never put off any of them. Angus Wilson was the only writer I know who wrote for posterity, not realising that time and changing taste made the decisions over the following years.

What are your ten essential classic novels for the next 100 years?

À la Recherche du Temps Perdu by Marcel Proust

Ulysses by James Joyce

The Trial by Frank Kafka

Brave New World by Aldous Huxley

Nineteen Eighty-four by George Orwell

To the Lighthouse by Virginia Woolf

Darkness at Noon by Arthur Koestler

A Passage to India by E. M. Forster

Midnight's Children by Salman Rushdie

Nostromo by Joseph Conrad

Each of the above would add to a young person's understanding and knowledge of human beings and of society in all its different aspects.

What are the books you believe should never have been called classics?

The Age of Reason trilogy by Jean-Paul Sartre. Originally seen as outstandingly innovative and philosophical fiction, it now creaks as it reads.

Lady Chatterley's Lover by D. H. Lawrence. The permissive age of the last two decades has made this seem thin and not remotely shocking in the way art should shock.

The Catcher in the Rye by J. D. Salinger. Eye- and mind-opener for the teenagers of the Sixties; thereafter declining in effect and kept alive only by the author successfully hiding from the world.

A Farewell to Arms by Ernest Hemingway. Much overrated from the word go and never likely to become a classic.

Gone with the Wind by Margaret Mitchell. Always a middlebrow, popular book that is unlikely to sustain its position as the years go by.

The above five have always had reputations beyond their deserts and these reputations are not unnaturally declining. I chose them because they were the first to come to mind and with a force that made me suspect the judgment to be not unfair.

MARTYN GOFF *is Administrator for the Booker Prize and the Chairman of Books For Keeps and the Poetry Book Society.*

Roy Hattersley

What is your definition of a classic?

Unfortunately 'classic' – used either as a noun or adjective – has a number of meanings, not all of which make the fiction to which it is applied attractive to the young. Like most grammar school boys of my generation, I read Austen, Dickens, Thackeray and Scott and if anyone told me that they were 'classic authors', it did not alter my judgment. I could find little or no merit in *Ivanhoe* and Mr Pickwick never made me laugh. But although I knew that both book and character were highly regarded – why else would they be on the syllabus? – my failure to enjoy them never made me feel inadequate. Now I am delighted that I was so discerning so young. *Ivanhoe* is on my list of books which have been (and perhaps still are) ridiculously overrated.

Nothing, I think, could have put me off Dickens – not least because my father had started reading it to me when I was five or six, beginning with *Martin Chuzzlewit*, a totally unsuitable book to read to a child. Austen I found more difficult. She *seemed* to write about a world which was diametrically different from mine. The idea that what she said had a universal quality was still ten years away. But neither the pleasure nor the pain had anything to do with the novelists' status as 'special'. Certainly if I had been asked what 'classic' meant, 'special' is what I would have replied. Perhaps these days we ought to speak of 'standards'. For the young, it would have a comforting association with the record industry. And, if I understand the term correctly, it represents exactly what 'classic' means in its most sensible form.

Clearly a classic has quality. So to use the term at all implies belief in some objective standard of literary excellence. Classics are listed in the canon – or one of the several canons – of English literature. They do not have to be in one of the sections of the general canon which we particularly enjoy. There is classic science fiction and there are classic detective stories, none of which I ever read. But classics are the best of their kind and, because they are so good, they last. *The Riddle of the Sands* and *The Secret Agent* are classics. The James Bond stories, although about more up-to-date espionage and naval intelligence, are not. A classic must be regarded, by people of judgment, as something worth reading fifty years after it was written. It is all to do with merit and nothing to do with fashion – though in literature, as in life, merit comes in many different forms.

What are your ten essential classic novels for the next 100 years?

The problem about listing ten classics is that the first couple of dozen are so obvious – *Middlemarch, Vanity Fair, Pride and Prejudice, Jane Eyre, Great Expectations, Wuthering Heights.* I have therefore confined my list to novels written since 1900, and listed ten novels which I believe, as well as possessing other merits, reveal something of the age about which they are written. Clearly, the more virtues a novel possesses, the more likely it is to be a classic. My 'Top Ten for the Twentieth Century' all help future generations to understand what the twentieth century was about:

Howard's End by E. M. Forster. The house as the world and the exposure of different people's attitudes towards it and therefore the values which they hold most dear. By far the best Forster.

The History of Mr Polly by H. G. Wells. Comic, sad, occasionally bizarre and one of the great examples of 'the little man' rising up against his oppressors.

Sons and Lovers by D. H. Lawrence. Early proof that the industrial poor also have complicated emotions and the best thing written about the tortured relationship only sons often have with demanding mothers.

The Great Gatsby by Scott Fitzgerald. Superficially about America in the Twenties but fundamentally about hope, despair and swimming against the tide. The narrator's return to Gatsby's house after Jay's death is as moving as anything written this century.

Brideshead Revisited by Evelyn Waugh. If the author really did regard it as inferior to the *Sword of Honour* trilogy, he was mistaken. It describes the yearning not for a world that is lost but for one which, although the characters do not know it, never existed.

Lucky Jim by Kingsley Amis. A book which provokes clichés though it does not contain one. I laughed aloud and could not put it down. Post-war provincial universities at their most hilarious.

Anglo-Saxon Attitudes by Angus Wilson. Picaresque novels were not in fashion in the mid-twentieth century, partly because they are so difficult to write well. Their essential quality is a collection of irresistible characters. *Anglo-Saxon Attitudes* has them.

Wide Sargasso Sea by Jean Rhys. Sequels are a difficult trick to perform well. Jean Rhys succeeds magnificently because she creates an appropriate air of mystery, intensified by the images of death and disaster.

Lord of the Flies by William Golding. An allegory for chaos, order and the innate brutality of authority. Also an interesting adventure story in its own right.

Midnight's Children by Salman Rushdie. The independence of India and Pakistan was, as well as a great historical event, both joy and trauma to millions of individuals. Rushdie writes about it as reality rather than headlines.

What are the books you believe should never have been called classics?

Ivanhoe by Walter Scott. A farrago of historical nonsense combined with maudlin romance.

Sybil by Benjamin Disraeli. Gothic extravaganza with absurd political message which is only remembered because Disraeli became Prime Minister.

A Shropshire Lad by A. E. Housman. Stories written in verse rarely work. *A Shropshire Lad* – which is certainly verse, not poetry – survives because it was somehow associated with the slaughter of the First World War.

Nineteen Eighty-four by George Orwell. Another lucky author. *Nineteen Eighty-four* was published in 1949, when the general public was beginning to be worried about the Soviet Union. Not to be compared with *Brave New World*.

The Thirty-nine Steps by John Buchan. Richard Hannay is so stupid that any half-witted German agent would have shot him by page 5.

The Jungle Book by Rudyard Kipling. A morality tale that gave worthless advice to children of the Empire.

Rasselas by Samuel Johnson. Unreadable now and probably unreadable in 1759. Still has nothing much to say of any great interest.

Around the World in Eighty Days by Jules Verne. The picaresque novel gone mad. The word had not been invented at the time but it is totally dependent on a gimmick.

Any two of Anthony Trollope's six 'Palliser' novels (*Can You Forgive Her?*, *Phineas Finn*, *The Eustace Diamonds*, *Phineas Redux*, *The Prime Minister* and *The Duke's Children*). Hardly a word about real politics. A few glimpses of parliamentary life do not make up for the general soap-opera quality.

ROY HATTERSLEY *is a novelist, journalist and writer and the former deputy leader of the Labour Party.*

Richard Hoggart

What is your definition of a classic?

My definition of a 'classic' novel is one which, through its splendid uses of language and its gifted perceptions into our experience, enthrals its own and succeeding generations. Those rather grand expressions contain, for me, the only sound reasons for a novel to last.

In the above sense, then, the term can be useful. But today its use is extremely muddled. On the one hand some people mistrust it because it sounds 'elitist', i.e. 'snob'. A foolish misconception hiding a fact such people do not want to face: that some books are better than others and that at any one time only a small number of people will break ranks, seek out and take the trouble to read 'classic' works. Most of us are content with the greatly-hyped contemporary and evanescent best-sellers, to which entry costs no trouble.

On the other hand the title 'classic' is handed out too freely, as a sort of compliment; to mean something that's lasted two or three decades and been rather influential. My own *The Uses of Literacy* is quite often introduced as 'a classic'. I do not accept the sloppy label; I return the bouquet.

As a child, obviously, I read some children's books, such as Percy F. Westerman and Richmal Crompton. I knew they were chiefly forms of entertainment and didn't despise them for that. But when (in a bookless home but at grammar school) I met Dickens and then Thackeray and so went on to Hardy and others, I knew I was in a more important world.

With some exceptions I would not recommend to children more than a few of the multitude of books which today target specific ages. I would prefer to encourage them to read *Alice in Wonderland, Robinson Crusoe, Gulliver's Travels, Pickwick Papers, Animal Farm* and the like. In short, there are classics which appeal to all ages at all times; and it is important, whatever else they read, to introduce children to them.

Incidentally, I reject the argument that it doesn't matter what you read as a child since any reading is good and can lead on and up to the better. Except for 0.5% or so of us, that is a deluded argument. Most of us don't go onwards and upwards. We go round and round and there's a lot of money to be made by those who provide that constantly replenished circular motion. They don't want us to get off the carousel.

A similar argument can be made against those who say TV adaptations often lead to a reading of the books themselves. But that's too long to go into here. I've written about it elsewhere. Look at the numbers of discarded 'TV classics' at car-boot sales.

No classic I was introduced to at school put me off good books. Quite the reverse. It takes more than even very bad teaching to put off a child, with a sense of language and a curiosity about life, from enjoying Shakespeare. Add for me writers such as Hardy, again, and Conrad and Forster and D. H. Lawrence; all met at school.

I don't know anyone who is writing 'with an eye to the twenty-first century'. I don't know what that phrase means. I suppose those who write deliberate pot-boilers might try to get on that wagon. The people I know write because they have to and some of them at all times have mused on this; e.g. Flaubert, Graham Greene, Kafka, etc, etc. And in my own small way I do too.

Some also have a sense of a hoped-for audience: 'fit audience tho' few', 'the ironic points of light', 'the saving remnant', 'the intelligent common reader' with whom Dr Johnson 'rejoiced to concur'. That's all got nothing to do with selling more and making more money.

The final sentence of paragraph one is incomprehensible to me for reasons which should now be clear. My kind of novelists don't have their eyes predominantly on the reader. The process is triangular: the writer looks at his or her experience and hopes it has been set down as he or she would best wish. Those are two points of the triangle. The third point is the reader who reads the resulting book but need not have direct contact with the author. There will be a sense of the author's personality, of course, but only through the book; and the author may have from responses to the book a sense of his or her readers. But there need be no direct author/reader relationship. To sum that up, the people I respect do not write 'to assure' a certain readership. They write so as to express the truth as they see it – as much as anything else, for their own sense of satisfaction, which may come from grappling with or playing with the truth. I am not much interested in other kinds of writer.

A further modern myth and attempted justification: that some books, which are widely read but disregarded by serious writers and readers, are nevertheless 'good of their kind'. Well, maybe. But do you see where that leads? That someone who sells adulterated food is good of his kind because he gets away with it? Or a successful prostitute? For those books which sell enormously but have little penetration into experience or gift of language we need another word, if we are not to reduce 'good' to 'anything that works'. True, some such books usually have to have some *effective* qualities or they wouldn't sell. You can't simply sit down and write a formulaic novel which will become a best-seller. You may have pace, but wooden characterisation. You may not see into any important aspects of life and describe them in a fitting language; but you may be able to elicit an 'ooh-ah' response in your readers. (You can fill in today's names of such writers for yourself). I would not call such books 'good' because in crucial ways they are anything but good. I would call them 'effective' (in their own restricted terms).

A further word in case the word 'elitist' is raising its ugly head now. Some books which tend to be dismissed by 'highbrows' have two important qualities which should be recognised and respected

(C. S. Lewis wrote well on this): 1. Even though in many ways (eg. plot) they may be conventional, they may in other ways honestly touch the heart, and that may be an important part of their wide appeal, e.g. Catherine Cookson. 2. Because of this they may rouse a genuine sense of common humane feeling beyond what the author may always be fully aware of.

What are your ten essential classic novels for the next 100 years?

If they really may be called 'classics', they are likely by definition to see out the next 100 years. There are of course far more than ten and I haven't time to put them in order. Some of Smollett, Fielding, Defoe (the main titles are obvious in each), Jane Austen (*Emma* will do for a start), the Brontës (*Jane Eyre* and *Wuthering Heights*), Thackeray, Trollope, George Eliot (I'd go for *Middlemarch*), Dickens, Hardy, Conrad (*Heart of Darkness*) and so on. But in the light of what I said above, such a list seems self-evident, obvious; any intelligent sixth-former could put it down. But if you want an odd, slightly less obvious name or two, I'd add *Tristram Shandy*, *The Way of All Flesh* and *Women in Love*. And so on and so on . . .

What are the books you believe should never have been called classics?

No, thanks. This part of the game I don't want to play. Simply too many names and titles occur which illustrate the contemporary muddle I've been talking about. Between those who hate the word 'classic' and those who give it out like a plastic medal there's no point in flogging dead horses of novels. In short, the word is then revealed, again, as often a form of fashionability. Who reads Charles Morgan now? Or Mary Webb, whose works Stanley Baldwin declared 'classics', or Uncle Tom Cobley . . . The climate of our age – probably of every age – makes us overpraise certain works which hit our particular nerves. The process of filtration ensures that when those particular nerves have lost their special temporal and temporary force, some works sink out of sight. This is different from saying that fashion may for two decades after death cause us to neglect an important author – e.g. GBS. He and others like him tend to come back. Enduring quality will out.

RICHARD HOGGART *is an academic and writer on contemporary culture. His many books include* The Uses of Literacy, An Imagined Life *and* The Way We Live Now.

Michael Holroyd

What is your definition of a classic?

I never think of novels as being 'classics' and I do not believe this is any longer a useful term. Most often, in recent years, it has been used by desperate marketing men and women in publishing houses who seldom have time to read the books they are promoting and who trust that the 'classic' label will somehow signal a prestige purchase. So it has become a lazy word, taken out and re-used whenever precise descriptive words are unforthcoming.

When I was young I associated Classics with school Latin: a dead language. At school I suspected most classic works of having grown dusty with age, of being imposed on young people by an older generation, on the living by the dead. At the sight of the word a violent prejudice would rise up in me. For I had been given a classic novel as the only prize I ever won. It was Walter Scott's *Quentin Durward*, an impenetrable historical romance set in fifteenth-century France. Written in the early nineteenth century, it was a veritable classic, I was told, that had lasted well into the mid-twentieth century. But not in my calendar it hadn't. It was a ridiculous novel to give a nine- or ten-year old. What I wanted was Rider Haggard's adventure story *She* or Conan Doyle's *The Lost World*. I should have been given Macaulay's *Lays of Ancient Rome* rather than, for God's sake, Wordsworth's 'Daffodils'. Those damn daffodils were a typical choice of my school. But undoubtedly they were classics, every one of them, all ten thousand. Now I see that it is a good poem: then it wasn't.

One quality that gives novels a natural long life is what Nabokov called 'enchantment'. It is a potent quality, but easily evades critical analysis and appears, like a flash of electricity, between the imagination of writer and reader in the magical act of reading. I also think some revolutionary ingredient is a good preservative in novels. And, of course, comedy. All imaginative work is humorous.

What are your ten essential classic novels for the next 100 years?

Since I don't believe there are such things as 'classic' novels, I can't really nominate one, let alone ten. But I can comment on my lack of nominations. What we need are fewer lists of best and best-selling novels, fewer best-of-the-best, fewer lists of prizes with their parades of winners and losers. What is appropriate for athletics is an absurdity for novel-writing, which cannot be judged by such simplified contests. We should stop awarding examination marks to novels and grow up. We depend too much on other people's choices and should cultivate our own confidence as readers.

What are the books you believe should never have been called classics?

There is only one novel I can't resist naming as a spectacular non-classic. It is, of course, Walter Scott's *Quentin Durward*.

MICHAEL HOLROYD *is the author of a number of biographies, including* Lytton Strachey, Augustus John *and* Bernard Shaw.

Shirley Hughes

What is your definition of a classic?

It seems impossible to write a satisfactory definition of a classic. Is it famous work of the past which you feel you ought to have read? Or some kind of universal voice transcending time and literary fashion? Getting onto a required O- or A-level reading list tends to give a book automatic classic status. Popular novels of the past, written for a non-literary audience who liked a good read, can become classics. Dickens wrote for such an audience. And Arnold Bennett, much patronised by the Bloomsbury set for being so readable and a good seller, is now certainly, and rightly, regarded as a classic author. Harper Lee, Raymond Chandler and P. G. Wodehouse have made it. It is an endlessly interesting game to speculate which contemporary popular fiction will be enshrined as a classic in the twenty-first century and which literary novels will disappear without trace.

With children's classics the term is constantly, but often falsely, bandied about. Mostly it has come to mean a book which has been highly regarded for a generation or more and probably enjoyed by adults too. Children, being not less intelligent than adults so much as inexperienced in life and readership, are only just beginning to find their way to an identification with fictional characters. We do this first of all, long before we can read, by looking at picture books and comic strips. Word and image are fused and are separated only when education takes over. It is no accident, therefore, that in some of the great children's classics the illustrator has a strong presence. The original images will survive, alongside the text, in spite of being plagiarised, Disneyfied and merchandised, to delight and terrify well into the next millennium.

A child's strong empathy with a fictional character tends to be first aroused by animals. Human identification comes later. Hence classics in all languages often feature anthropomorphic animals as symbols and, of course, as children and grown-ups in disguise. Real animals are thinner on the ground. Children can be so painfully agonised by a fictional animal lost or cruelly treated that the story will be remembered throughout life, though it may not be first-class writing at all. But they can also be a very tough, dispassionate audience who can readily cope with the big classic themes of love and death.

So many times we are told that authors of children's classics wrote not for children but to please themselves, or that they were mysteriously more in touch with the child within themselves than other writers. This seems to be rather an overworked observation. It is certainly true, in reading biographies of children's authors, that you often come across a big bang of some kind (though not necessarily an unhappy one) in their early lives. Sometimes a bad trauma like the loss of a parent, but perhaps an illness which required being alone a lot, away from the company of other children, or being taken out of a familiar place and dumped down in a strange one where they became outside observers. The feeling of being that age becomes crystallised in the memory. The pattern on a carpet or wallpaper opens up magically, a small back garden becomes a wonderland.

Children's writers, even the great ones, walk a perilous tightrope between sentiment in its true sense and sentimentality. They must evoke all the power of the story in fewer, simpler sentences and strong imagery. They were among the first to use the grammar of the cinema. Of all writing forms, at its best it is probably one of the most durable and influential.

Required Reading?

In a pre-television, wartime childhood, as mine was, there was plenty of time to read. There were a lot of books about, but even so my reading was based on the principle that if you got hold of a really good one you might as well stick to it. Which I did, endlessly re-reading old favourites and finding the repetition delightful rather than tiresome. I also favoured the ventilated page. The sight of pages of close print unrelieved by illustrations was truly offputting.

So I incline towards the view that to force-feed younger children 'classics' is probably a mistake. The trouble with grown-ups trying to get children to read them is that they (the grown-ups) have often forgotten what the books are actually like. It is not uncommon for an adult to embark upon reading a classic aloud only to find that it is not what they imagined it to be at all. To skip or not to skip – that is the question. Plus, offstage, much anxious, surreptitious perusing of shortened editions, re-tellings and strip-cartoon versions. But by then it is too late. You've lost your audience. Oldies with fond recollections of being curled up with *Swiss Family Robinson* had better watch their step.

In my teens I became much more adventurous. Then I could have done with more skilled advice in the form of enthusiastic recommendation rather than required reading, plus some judicious reading aloud. The weekly Saturday afternoon visit to the public library was an institution, though there was no special children's section and the books, both adult and children's, wore the same uniform maroon or dark green bindings. It was just a question of working your way along the shelf from Hans Andersen through (in my case past) *The Children of the New Forest* and *Lorna Doone* until you found yourself in the company of Evelyn Waugh, Theodore Dreiser and J. B. Priestley.

We read books, as all children do, as a way of finding out more about Life, and more particularly about the mysteries of the opposite sex (more of a mystery then than it is today). A few classics slipped under my guard which filled the bill very well. At home I do

not remember being urged to read anything in particular because it
was 'good' literature, or being censured when I was going through a
phase of not reading much at all because I was getting all the
thrilling narrative I needed from the cinema. At school, of course,
we read Shakespeare, Chaucer, the Romantic Poets (large chunks
learned by heart), Restoration drama, Homer in translation and the
Bible Stories. We did not analyse them as children are required to
do today. They just came up like the mid-morning milk and we
paddled about in them. I have never ceased to be grateful.

The problem is that today, in the hectic life of modern childhood,
leaving children to form their own reading taste doesn't always
work. There simply isn't time to wade in. So, like all grandparents, I
long for every child to encounter a gifted teacher who will open
doors, will get them to persevere with books which require some
measure of patience and imaginative concentration, rather than to
be so afraid of boring them to even try. It is a lot to ask, a heroic
endeavour.

Writers for children today have to be entertaining from the first
paragraph or go under. There is such a fear of losing the reader to
some other diversion that it has to be crash, bang, wallop, into the
exciting bit in the opening sentence. The idea is to do that and write
like a dream. Robert Louis Stevenson managed it, after all.

Homer For

Reading Homer's *The Iliad* and *The Odyssey* in translation at school
was a great piece of good fortune. I would never have picked it up
and read it of my own accord. But being brought to it, reading it
carefully and thoughtfully with a good teacher, was a revelation. I
will always remember it as a series of vividly-lit pictures. And I can
return to it now and then, taking it on various levels, always
surprised and delighted rather than (as might have happened)
approaching it for the first time with awe and trepidation. Or worse,
never at all.

All this comes down to encountering someone who pulls down

the barriers for you. I do hope such people will go on trying. Finding Homer so enjoyable gave me the confidence to read Virgil's *The Aeneid* in Robert Fitzgerald's wonderful translation. If I survive until the year 2020, when it is predicted there will be an overwhelming number of old people, no doubt washed up in retirement homes gazing at TV ads and afternoon chat shows, it is a comfort to know that if I close my eyes those pictures, created so long ago, will still be there.

The future of many nineteenth- and early twentieth-century classics may possibly lie with audio tapes. Children certainly come to many books they would not read to themselves in this way and so do adults. Does it matter that it's not print but a voice, heard lying in the dark or driving along in your car? I don't think so. We all belonged to an oral storytelling culture once, after all.

Dickens Against

I am profoundly grateful that Dickens was not forced upon me as a child. Now, I find reading him one of the great pleasures of later life. Half-hearted attempts were made to interest me in children's versions but the effect was mostly one of gloom and terror. The stunning style, the humour, the marvellous patterns of plot eluded you, and you were left with the cruelty. And Dickens is so good at cruelty, especially to children. To be forced to identify with Oliver Twist or David Copperfield or poor Smike was just too awful to be borne.

With Dickens the pictures in the head, as well as on the page, are essentially in black and white. They have an engraved quality and are full of looming shadows and grotesques. Hablot Browne's illustrations, though brilliant, may not appeal in the next century. They are over-detailed at the expense of atmosphere. Or rather, they have an atmosphere but it is not quite the right one. Perhaps some towering Daumier of the future will emerge to meet the challenge. Or, as one sometimes feels about the beautifully photographed television versions, do we need the pictures at all?

Those in the head are probably better, if we have not been made into a visually punch-drunk society by then.

If Dickens is going to be read aloud to children we need good edited versions, such as those by Grace Hogarth (now sadly out of print) rather than mere re-tellings. The opening chapter of *Great Expectations* will continue to grab any reader. But forcing the tender-hearted child through the horrors of Dotheboys Hall is a more dubious endeavour.

What are your ten essential classic novels for the next 100 years?

Children's

If the definition of a children's classic is that it should have enormous appeal over a long period of time, then Roald Dahl and Enid Blyton clearly lead the field. But more profound characterisation may yet win the day. No apologies are offered for the following highly traditional choice – the illustrative opportunities are simply irresistible:

Treasure Island by Robert Louis Stevenson. Stevenson has a stunning prose style. He also rivets the reader's attention from page to page, keeping the story going at full belt. And he has created one of the most memorable characters in children's literature: Long John Silver, that most charming of villains, the man 'with a face as big as a ham plain and pale but intelligent and smiling', who can turn from affability to murderous rage but still leaves you half hoping that he survives to settle down in comfort, in this world if not the next. If any illustrations survive also I hope they are Mervyn Peake's.

Huckleberry Finn by Mark Twain. A first-person narrative by the archetypal bad boy, who sits so powerfully in the American psyche. This book has an enormous dark power which its pair, *Tom Sawyer*, never quite achieves. Anyone who dismisses it on the grounds that Huck's white-trash attitude to Jim, the runaway slave, stamps this subtle narrative as merely ignominiously racist should read Toni

Morrison's wonderful ambivalent essay on her own reaction to this book. Much better without illustrations.

The Story of Babar, the Little Elephant by Jean de Brunhoff. It encompasses, in infant terms, all the big themes: death, family, marriage and shopping. On only the second spread Babar's mother is shot by a cruel hunter. I seem to remember my four-year-old son reading this bit aloud to me with particular relish. Of course, we both knew that almost immediately Babar would meet a kind old lady 'who understood little elephants' and gave him her purse. De Brunhoff's seemingly artless style in both writing and drawing is masterly: simple flat colour, a wonderfully lively line in a style which is closely related to the best French *bande dessinée* tradition. The large-format editions are essential to the true flavour. Babar and family will certainly march confidently into the next century.

The Tintin Books by Hergé. Hergé has been called the Homer of the strip cartoon. His characters are quotably original, his draughtsmanship dazzling. Probably, for the insular British, our best hope of learning a European language at an early age.

Winnie-the-Pooh and *The House at Pooh Corner* by A. A. Milne. A. A. Milne's Pooh books are unique. The nostalgic appeal of a little boy in a smock inhabiting an upper-class nursery, told with the gentle facetious address to children so fashionable in that era, will recede, of course – it is already light years away from modern childhood – but what is left will still emerge as a lasting classic. Mostly because the characters are so memorable and the oblique conversations so funny. Ernest Shepard's illustrations are an essential ingredient of this phenomenal success. It is no surprise that, Disney travesty aside, no illustrator has had the nerve to try a re-interpretation. Shepard's deceptively slight, relaxed line and his enormous charm are underpinned by formidable powers of draughtsmanship. He has an uncanny skill in breathing life into inanimate stuffed toys, giving them that worn look of having been a good deal toted about. The way the drawings are so artlessly dropped into the text on each spread is in itself a good justification for the survival of a book as a lasting form of entertainment. And he sets the stories so impeccably, with the wind fairly whistling through the trees of the Ashdown Forest.

Milne has an airy lightness of touch which many children's writers try to emulate but which is so hard to achieve. (He is a dab hand at light verse too). The wit always counteracts the winsomeness. The appeal on many levels, to every age-group, is one of sheer dazzling class and style.

Alice's Adventures in Wonderland and *Through the Looking Glass* by Lewis Carroll. These are classics which all children think they have read but quite a lot haven't. They should be read aloud, preferably before the Disney version kicks in. Tenniel's images are indelible. Their quality is so closely associated with the story that it is impossible to imagine Lewis Carroll being originally teamed with another illustrator. Many have risen to the challenge since, from Arthur Rackham to Barry Moser, but none has eclipsed or matched that memorable combination. Tenniel's characterisation of Alice herself is essentially dreamlike, the little entranced face under that huge bush of hair. It is curiously at variance with the level-headed little girl in the story, who manages such a down-to-earth, sensible response to the wildly surrealistic logic of the characters with whom she has to contend. Yet in our memories the two merge. The pictures in *Through the Looking Glass* in which Alice and the Sheep are gliding in their rowing boat on the dark water while the background melts into the lighted toyshop, is as expressive of dreaming as any image I know. Heralded by its great fame, *Alice* will be regarded as a classic far into the future, and quite right too.

Adult

A Handful of Dust by Evelyn Waugh. Lasting humour is probably one of the highest achievements for a writer and the most difficult. Waugh's humour in this, the wryest, coldest, most brilliant of his novels, is the twentieth-century kind. There is so little physical description, it is so spare and bleak, the subtlety is in the subtext of the conversations.

Three love stories which turn on a powerful sexual passion, sustained throughout with no explicit love scene at all:

Anna Karenina by Leo Tolstoy

Victory by Joseph Conrad

A Man Could Stand Up by Ford Madox Ford

Neglected Classics

Clever Bill by William Nicholson. A brilliant piece. Sendak regards it, alongside *The Pirate Twins,* as a perfect balance of word and image. Nicholson has used limited lithographed colour with a black line rather than his better-known woodcut technique. The minimal odyssey of Mary's toy soldier, who gets left out of the suitcase when she goes on a visit but valiantly runs after the train and makes it just in time to meet her on the platform at Dover, never fails to grip three- and four-year olds. Why, oh why, is it out of print?

Mary Plain books by Gwyneth Rae. One of the funniest and most original Bear characters. Mary is an orphan, born in the Bear Pits at Berne, though her anthropomorphic exploits mostly take place in a highly recognisable 1930's London in the company of her human guardian, the bespectacled Owl Man. Mary's rebus picture letters are a delight. Her exuberance, charm, wilfulness, greed and occasional lapses into homesickness are all too recognisable. Happily two of this series have recently been brought back into print.

The Once and Future King by T. H. White. Not many children read Malory these days. But if the Arthurian legend is going to live on – and it is a good bet that it will – their re-telling is essential reading.

Authors for the twenty-first century:

Ian McEwan
Saul Bellow
Raymond Briggs
Kate Atkinson
Philip Pullman
John Banville
James Lasdun

Writers who, variously, use movie grammar, can create sweepingly-lit, powerfully dramatic scenes, who deal in parallel worlds which run very close to our own shabby recognisable one rather than fantasy ones in outer space (surely old hat by the year 2000?), who can intermesh word and image, and can take the strip-cartoon format seriously enough to use it as a vehicle for subtle narrative, whose humour has lasting appeal.

Above all, any author who can brilliantly succeed in creating a good, happy character yet still rivet the reader's attention. Villains, the neurotic, look-at-me attention grabbers, are so much more vivid and memorable than saints. Happiness is so hard to write about. Misery, unfortunately, is much easier.

What are the books you believe should never have been called classics?

Children's

The *Narnia* books by C. S. Lewis. As religion will undoubtedly be a great force in the next century, people may be increasingly repelled by Lewis's hijacking of the crucifixion and resurrection of Christ to reinforce the emotional impact of the Aslan character. The under-lying elements of lugubrious guilt may also be unacceptable to adults. But these books are so readable that to most children all this is simply water off a duck's back.

Peter Pan in Kensington Gardens by J. M. Barrie. Barrie's play *Peter Pan* exercises a perennial fascination, and children will always respond to its irresistible dramatic ingredients. But anyone revisiting the book *Peter Pan in Kensington Gardens* is in for a nasty shock. It exudes a neurotic sentimentality about the state of infancy. The story, in which baby Peter, who can remember his pre-natal state of being a bird, flies out of his nursery window into the Gardens to live with the other birds and fairies and returns to find the window barred, and his mother caressing a new baby in his place in the cot, reveals the core of Barrie's obsession with never growing up. Because mothers always betray you.

Adult

The Forsyte Saga by John Galsworthy. My parents' generation would not have hesitated to rate these novels high in a list of classics. Now they are out of style. Perhaps it is because, against such a solid and detailed background, Soames is the only character who stands out as fully three-dimensional. Or perhaps because the heroine, Irene, is so infuriating to most female readers that they can't get through to the end without longing for her knicker elastic to suddenly give way at some exquisitely gracious moment.

SHIRLEY HUGHES *is a prolific and award-winning children's author and illustrator.*

John Humphrys

What is your definition of a classic?

I have always distrusted the word 'classic' when it's attached to a novel. There are good books and bad books and, very occasionally, great books. A novel must stand the test of time and still be read enthusiastically generations after it was written for it to qualify for the dubious distinction of 'classic'. That is the only objective measurement: longevity. Everything else is subjective.

In my own (highly subjective) view, too many novels that are eventually called 'classics' are written as an exercise in self-indulgence. They may be admired by clever literary folk and receive wonderful reviews, but are then largely unread. So I would regard *Middlemarch* as a truly great novel – it passes the test of longevity, is beautifully written, enriches the human spirit, and is immensely readable – but not, for instance, *Tristram Shandy*. I simply did not enjoy it and therefore did not want to read it. For me it failed the critical test.

I did not read the classics as a child, except those required for O-levels, and I'm not sorry about that. It was good to come fresh to Eliot and Austen and Trollope and read them because I wanted to, not because I had to. I suspect I would have found Trollope, in particular, boring as a child. Reading him after many years of reporting the political scene meant I could put his characters and their dubious behaviour in context. You discover that politicians really have not changed throughout the ages. For better or for worse.

Instead the young Humphrys read American authors like Hemingway, Faulkner and Steinbeck. Wonderful reading for a teenager. I can still taste the dust of Hemingway's *corridas* and smell the fish of Steinbeck's *Cannery Row*. I have returned to them all in later life and most of them are still wonderful reading. I read Graham Greene as a youngster, too, and read him still.

What are your ten essential classic novels for the next 100 years?

To select ten essential classics is impossible for all those reasons, but here are some that have already passed my own test – the test of time and readability – and others that will, I believe, still be read generations from now.

Middlemarch and *The Mill on the Floss* by George Eliot

Pride and Prejudice by Jane Austen

Great Expectations by Charles Dickens

The Small House at Allington by Anthony Trollope (but *Phineas Finn* if it's politics you're after)

One Hundred Years of Solitude by Gabriel Garcia Marquez

Of Mice and Men by John Steinbeck (scarcely a novel, but a simple story beautifully told)

For Whom the Bell Tolls by Ernest Hemingway (he's out of fashion in these politically correct, sensitive times, but will return)

The Power and the Glory by Graham Greene

Cold Mountain by Charles Frazier (I had never heard of him until I read this, his first novel. He is a natural; a storyteller who writes with astonishing power and leaves you deeply moved. If it is not read for many years to come, then there ain't no justice.)

What are the books you believe should never have been called classics?

I won't nominate ten books that I believe should never have been called classics. If enough people think they are, then they are.

JOHN HUMPHRYS *is a radio and television broadcaster. His book,* Who Cares? The State of Britain, *is published in the spring of 1999.*

Patrick Janson-Smith

What are your ten essential classic novels for the next 100 years?

Can't do a list of classics that shouldn't have been called classics, 'cos if they've been labelled thus, they is! But here are my 'Top Ten Classics'. Of course, it's really only a list of those books that I can remember having enjoyed hugely and would read again and again, if I had but time:

Tess of the D'Urbervilles by Thomas Hardy

Little Dorrit by Charles Dickens

A Handful of Dust by Evelyn Waugh

The Magic Pudding by Norman Lindsay

The Picture of Dorian Gray by Oscar Wilde

Keep the Aspidistra Flying by George Orwell

The Diary of a Nobody by George and Weedon Grossmith

Three Men in a Boat by Jerome K. Jerome

England, Their England by A. G. McDonnell

A Prayer for Owen Meany by John Irving

The dictionary defines 'classic' as being of the first class, of acknowledged excellence; remarkably typical; outstandingly important. My definition of classic – i.e. as defined by the list of books above – is obstinately rooted in the belief that the best literature is

that which you carry in your heart from the moment you read it to
the moment you die.

PATRICK JANSON-SMITH *is the Publisher, Adult Trade Books at the
publishers Transworld.*

Elizabeth Jennings

What is your definition of a classic?

When I was at school, a classic meant a novel that was difficult to read or to get into. Thus the early chapters of Scott's historical novels can be skipped without much loss. Jane Austen I liked because she goes straight into her stories. Of course much of her social wit is lost on a child, but I liked Darcy in *Pride and Prejudice* because he was so stand-offish! I don't much care for the word classic and would rather reserve it for Latin and Greek texts.

The only contemporary novelist who I feel has an eye on the future is Anthony Powell in his long sequence *A Dance to the Music of Time*. Save for one or two characters, such as the musician Moreland, the novels give me little pleasure. I find them over-elaborate and rather unsubtle.

What are your ten essential classic novels for the next 100 years?

Lucky Jim by Kingsley Amis remains as funny as it was when published half a century ago. The humour is hilarious without ever being unkind and infectious without ever being dark. Jim is drawn in the round and we quickly like him and are glad when, in spite of all his misadventures, everything turns out well for him. This is enduring humour.

The Great Gatsby by F. Scott Fitzgerald must surely be one of the very few fine novellas written in English (or American) this century. Fitzgerald is a Romantic but one whose prose style is economical and judicious. Gatsby is one of those Romantic figures (the great prototype is, of course, Dante) who falls in love with a girl he has only seen once. He becomes rich in order to give her everything. The plot of this novella is ingenious and beautifully designed. The whole short story has a 'romantic readiness', Fitzgerald's own phrase. There is nothing fulsome here.

A Passage to India is E. M. Forster's finest novel. This is mainly because his prevailing theme in all his novels – the opposition between the enlightened heart and the chilly intellect – is in India found naturally. Forster is far too subtle a writer to present us with a direct conflict; the Anglo-Indians are not all unsympathetic. The prose is, of course, peerless.

Brighton Rock by Graham Greene. Here, as in all his novels, Greene is deeply concerned with evil and guilt. The young protagonist, the cruel Pinky, is almost frightening. This book would have endured anyway but it has an extra potency now because, in this torn, materialist end of the century, we see and hear about young men as wicked as Pinky all too frequently. Greene's easy, straightforward prose manifests the art that conceals art.

Somerset Maugham's *The Razor's Edge* is a late novel and one of his finest, perhaps the finest. *Of Human Bondage* is a magnificent account of a young man's obsessive love for a girl he knows is worthless, but its prose is not so splendidly unadorned as that of *The Razor's Edge*. In the latter, Maugham takes on one of the hardest tasks a novelist can set himself. He creates a totally convincing good person. Larry Darrell flew in World War One and returns to Chicago (Maugham knows his USA well) determined to find out the meaning of life. This sounds off-putting but, in fact, Larry is a delightful, witty, kind and extremely intelligent man. On his quest he travels through much of Europe and then finds what he wants in India. Elliott Templeton, second in importance only to Larry, is a magnificent example of a great snob who is also a kind and generous man. Though never out of print, Maugham has never really been considered a great writer. In *The Razor's Edge* he is and here his prose is very fine, easy but not facile, spare but not empty. *The Razor's Edge* is a masterpiece.

The Catcher in the Rye by J. D. Salinger is written in the first person by an American adolescent schoolboy who has run away from school. Holden Caulfield is a 'mixed-up kid' but a very lovable one. We learn compassion from him even while he arouses ours. Salinger's prose moves fast but there are no clichés here. Every detail of thought, emotion and location is illuminating. It is the work of a genius.

The Conscience of the Rich by C. P. Snow is out of print in paperback and hardback. This is surely extraordinary. Snow's prose varies and can be commonplace. At its best it serves him well. He is important because he knew intimately so many worlds – the academic, the scientific, Parliament, the Civil Service. The long sequence of books called *Strangers and Brothers* is uneven in quality. Each book was intended to be read on its own. Some novels deal deftly with one aspect of British life but some ase wholly devoted to one character. *The Conscience of the Rich* is devoted to a rich Anglo-Jewish family. Charles, the son of the house, is at odds with his father, called by him and his sister 'Mr L'. Charles could be a successful barrister but chooses to do a valuable but not particularly lucrative job – to be an ordinary doctor, a GP. This is a remarkable and beautifully written book (at his worst, Snow can be repetitive and slapdash) and its vivid portrait of English Jews and their world is of extraordinary merit.

To the Lighthouse by Virginia Woolf is an experimental novel; it resembles an extended prose poem. But this experiment is always lucid and comprehensible. Unlike James Joyce, who plundered and altered English language and literature in *Ulysses,* Woolf is easy to read. Her innovation lies in the fact that her plot and characters in *To the Lighthouse* are subservient to the elements, the tides and all the forces of Nature. Woolf's prose is rich and flowing; it gives us the feeling of the pulse and energy of life itself. Woolf writes fastidiously and her style is very beautiful.

I believe without any doubt at all that Evelyn Waugh is the greatest novelist of this century. He never wrote a bad book; his first one, *Decline and Fall*, is written with economy, humour and feeling for character. I am choosing three others in order to do justice to his genius – *Scoop, Put Out More Flags* and Waugh's last great fictional work, the *Sword of Honour* trilogy.

Scoop makes a farce out of Fleet Street, a newspaper called *The Daily Beast* and its proprietor who is named Lord Copper. The wonderfully controlled, farcical plot concerns a confusion between two contributors called Boot. The one who usually writes the paper's Nature Notes is sent abroad as a foreign correspondent to cover an imminent war. This plot is sustained most skilfully and Waugh never fails to produce his comic inventiveness.

Put Out More Flags is about what the 'Bright Young Things' do when the 1939 war breaks out. It is a tragie-comedy and contains, in its depiction of three young evacuees, a comic event that is as successful as Jane Austen's 'Collins Letter'. It is a joy, as is the whole novel.

In the *Sword of Honour* trilogy, the three novels are called *Men at Arms, Officers and Gentlemen* and *Unconditional Surrender*. Here, seriousness is implicit. Nonetheless, there are countless comic characters and incidents. The protagonist, Guy Crouchback, is a very likable man who spends much time being promoted and demoted in the Army. The huge gallery of characters is as rich as anything written by Dickens. The serious element, which moves easily along with hilarious humour, is about Christian love and salvation. Guy's father, old Crouchback, is almost a saint but a charming and completely convincing one. Great comic characters include Apthorpe and Guy's commanding officer, named Ritchie-Hook. Cowards such as the effete Ivor Claire mingle with sinister characters such as Corporal-Major Ludovic. As in his other novels, Waugh is never at a loss for names (another Dickensian gift). If Waugh had not written the *Sword of Honour* trilogy he would probably have been only an exceptionally fine novelist. As it is, Evelyn Waugh shows undisputed genius. Every novel he wrote absorbs and delights the reader.

What are the books you believe should never have been called classics?

About novels which are considered 'classics' – e.g. anything by Sterne, Fielding, Smollett, Jane Austen, Scott, Dickens, Thackeray, Hardy, to name obvious authors – I think that, in general, novels which are still in print, by any of these and other authors, are surely classics. A year or two ago, my publisher invited me to make a personal anthology of poetry. I found, almost always, that time itself has usually proved the best judge, so that if I tried to choose less obvious poems by, for example, Donne or Wordsworth, I was usually wrong. That is all I feel is worth saying on this matter. For me the same applies to past fiction.

ELIZABETH JENNINGS *is a highly acclaimed poet who has been awarded a C.B.E. for her services to poetry.*

A. L. Kennedy

What is your definition of a classic?

A classic, in my opinion would be a book which in some manner celebrates and encourages the human imagination, which renders possible the impossible, which sustains the interior life of the reader and which speaks to and of the human spirit.

Whether the modern definition of 'classic' is anything other than fashion- and finance-led I wouldn't know. Equally, some of the accepted 'classics' may not have done anything other than make a handful of academics feel they've found something suitably obscure and unreadable to bolster their own high opinion of their thought processes over those of the common mass.

Having said this, when I was younger, I dosed myself with a variety of classics as if they were patent medicines for the brain – Shakespeare, Wordsworth, Dante, Milton, Boccaccio, Homer, Virgil and so forth. Largely, I found that after an initial demand of effort they left me regularly exultant and nourished. Because I was reading them privately, I also had no need for contact with any kind of critical interpretation or other interference. No one ever told me that they were not my inheritance, my right. They were a deeply democratic and personal joy. They also gave me the pleasure of walking into a public library and saying that I was looking for *Paradise Lost*, which I was then given. It's never got any easier than that.

What are your ten essential classic novels for the next 100 years?

I provide a list with the rider that my own list would be different tomorrow and lists are invidious.

Moby Dick by Herman Melville. A deeply spiritual book, wonderfully written, pleasantly eccentric, humanely messy, ultimately triumphant. Its attempt to address the conflict between man and nature and man and God remains timeless.

Dr Jekyll and Mr Hyde by R. L. Stevenson. Again, a beautifully crafted book, full of a controlled passion, an understanding of humanity and a rage against hypocrisy.

Catch-22 by Joseph Heller. A wonderful picture of the insanity man is capable of creating and finding a home for within an unsentimental condemnation of war. Carefully and powerfully written, with characters who continue to provide models for more contemporary figures.

That Hideous Strength by C. S. Lewis. A mind that you wouldn't want to be without. A very fine book with a dreadful title, this shows a chilling understanding of the mechanisms of destruction and a strong grasp of the powers beyond the mundane. A successful mingling of the strengths of many older storytelling traditions from a man who believed in the power of story. Also a book with a notably savage conclusion.

Player Piano by Kurt Vonnegut. Another mind to keep around for the next century. In this book he creates a fictional world which reflects consistently on mankind's inability to be human, on the products of personal fear and the dangers and delights of personal freedom and simple loving kindness.

An Invincible Memory by Joao Ubaldo Ribeiro. A triumph of magical realism, a history lesson, a celebration of linguistic possibility, and a testament to the strength of humanity and its ability to preserve its better nature in the midst of chaos and barbarity.

The Third Policeman by Flann O'Brien. A wonderful, funny, heart-breaking nightmare of a book. A fiction which delights in its fictionality and which bores into the brain with far more force than fact.

Athena by John Banville. Marvellously crafted writing holding a beautiful and entirely convincing depiction of dangerous obsession, self-wounding passion and guilt.

Confessions of a Justified Sinner by James Hogg. An astute, wickedly funny and enduringly relevant dissection of personal morality which forces language and construction to the limits in a disturbingly fascinating journey towards somewhere very like Hell.

A Trail of Heart's Blood Wherever We Go by Robert Olmstead. A mystifyingly neglected book full of tenderness, longing and dark humour. Above human affairs, larger concerns and a beautifully evoked landscape loom, giving the book a genuinely numinous quality.

What are the books you believe should never have been called classics?

I can only reflect my personal taste. If Virginia Woolf is now regarded as 'classic' I have to say she leaves me mainly cold. Jane Austen doesn't do a huge amount for me. Much of Wordsworth, much of Tennyson and around fifty per cent of T. S. Eliot don't ring my bell, either. Ho hum.

A. L. KENNEDY *is the author of three collections of short stories and two novels,* Looking for the Possible Dance *and* So I Am Glad.

Francis King

What is your definition of a classic?

In the course of a lifetime one's friendships shift up and down, sometimes so slowly that one is hardly aware of what is happening and sometimes so abruptly that one suffers a stab, either of dismay if the movement is downwards, or of delight if it is upwards. Often, after a friendship has shifted to rock bottom and, in effect, died, it would clearly be better to abandon it. Some people resolutely, even ruthlessly, do this. Others, like myself, vainly hope that somehow it will be possible to restore it to life.

What is true of friendships in the course of a lifetime is also true of classics in the history of a culture. Books yo-yo up and down in esteem, and it is those which are more often in a high position than in a low one over a period of decades or even centuries which eventually come to be regarded as classics. But just as relationships often continue to be regarded as friendships long after they are, in fact, either moribund or dead, so books often continue to be cherished as classics long after only a handful of people have any inclination to read them.

Every dedicated reader must have his or her list of fiction classics which fall into this category of living dead. For me, such a list would immediately take in both Samuel Richardson's *Pamela* and his *Clarissa*. Who nowadays wants to read the literally hundreds of pages which detail, in letters of a length so inordinate that neither heroine could have had time to do anything other than compose them, a woman's struggles to preserve her virginity? My list would also, more

controversially, take in the novels of Walter Scott – described by
Hazlitt as 'lord of the ascendant', which indeed he was at a time
when writers all over Europe were producing even more tedious
historical romances in his manner, but who bored me when I was a
schoolboy and who bores me even more excruciatingly now. Yet
more controversial is my rejection of Dickens. His energy was
phenomenal – how, without the aid of a typewriter, let alone a word-
processor, did he manage to write all those marvellous letters while
leading a life of unremitting social and literary activity? No less
phenomenal was his ingenuity in constructing an elaborate plot.
But Agatha Christie possessed those same two gifts, as does Ruth
Rendell today. Trollope was right when he said that, though 'Mrs
Gamp, Micawber, Pecksniff and others have become household
words, as though they were human beings . . . they are not really
human beings . . . but puppets.' Also in my list are Cervantes's *Don
Quixote*, George Eliot's *Silas Marner*, Bulwer-Lytton's *The Last Days of
Pompeii* and Charles Kingsley's *Westward Ho!*.

All too often novels are regarded as potential classics because of
the influence which they exert on their readers at the time of their
first appearance and not because of any intrinsic greatness. Obvious
examples of such books are William Godwin's *Caleb Williams*
(socialism), Harriet Beecher Stowe's *Uncle Tom's Cabin* (black-white
relations), Mrs Humphry Ward's *Robert Elsmere* (religious doubt)
and H. G. Wells's *Anna Veronica* (feminism).

Sometimes a writer produces both a novel which will never
become a classic despite its wide-spread influence and a book which
is potentially a classic even though it has no influence at all. So
Aldous Huxley produced both the highly influential *Brave New World*
and the delightful, totally un-influential *Antic Hay*; and André Gide
both *Corydon*, a book of huge influence on all educated homo-
sexuals in the immediate aftermath of its publication but seen to be
of scant literary merit today, and *Les faux-monnayeurs*, a diamond of a
book, hard and sparkling, which has probably exerted no influence
on anyone not a writer. Other novels which have had a huge
influence but which are unlikely to be established as classics in the

twenty-first century are George Orwell's *Nineteen Eighty-four,* James Baldwin's *Another Country,* and a lot of books recently acclaimed in the often raucous feminist canon.

What are your ten essential classic novels for the next 100 years?

The Tale of Genji by Lady Murasaki, the first of all novels and in my view one of the greatest.

Fielding's *Tom Jones,* which Gibbon prophesied would 'outlast the Escorial and the eagles of Austria', and which I love for its humanity, its humour and its total lack of cant.

Balzac's *La Cousine Bette,* though many other volumes in his astonishing *La Comédie Humaine* deserve also to be included.

Dostoevsky's *The Brothers Karamazov,* for its mastery of political and religious ideas and its shattering insights into morbid psychology.

Stendhal's *La Chartreuse de Parme,* prodigal in the thrilling variety of its closely observed characters.

Proust's *À la Recherche du Temps Perdu,* which repeatedly demonstrates how a great artist can plunder the hidden store of the unconscious to tremendous effect.

Joseph Conrad's *Heart of Darkness,* the best of all short fictions and the masterpiece of the greatest writer in English of this century.

Thackeray's *Vanity Fair,* one of the few novels which I have read many times with increasing pleasure.

Charlotte Brontë's *Jane Eyre,* a magnificent depiction of the triumph of selfless love.

Tolstoy's *War and Peace,* by general consent the greatest novel of them all.

By writers of my own lifetime, I should nominate the following ten novels as being most likely eventually to achieve classic status in the century ahead:

Manservant and Maidservant by Ivy Compton-Burnett

A Passage to India by E. M. Forster

A Dance to the Music of Time by Anthony Powell

A Farewell to Arms by Ernest Hemingway

Lolita by Vladimir Nabokov

The Magic Mountain by Thomas Mann

The Unbearable Lightness of Being by Milan Kundera

A Bend in the River by V. S. Naipaul

Herzog by Saul Bellow

The Cancer Ward by Alexander Solzhenitsyn

If any contemporary novelist is deliberately writing for the twenty-first century, then his efforts are futile. A writer should not write for any specific readership, much less for a century. He should write for himself or for God if (as I do not) he believes in His existence.

FRANCIS KING'S *many novels include* The Woman who Was God, A Hand at the Shutter *and* Dead Letters.

Cosmo Landesman

What is your definition of a classic?

My definition of a classic novel:

A classic novel is a timeless read that I never have time to read.

Classic novels are the ones sitting on my shelf that tell other people that I'm a well-read chap.

Classic novels are the ones sitting on my shelf that tell me I'm a fraud for never having read them.

Classic novels are books I promise I will read come tomorrow. And when tomorrow comes, tomorrow will do.

Classic novels remind me that I once had a life of the mind; now I have a mindless life of magazines and media.

In my teens, I used to actually read classic novels all the time. And I was proud to be seen with classic novels. I proudly carried around Penguin paperbacks in my back pocket for everyone to see. In retrospect I realise that showing off my bum was an odd way to show people I had a good mind.

Back then I thought that girls would be impressed with a guy who read Jean-Paul Sartre and Kafka. And they were. But for some reason they always slept with the cute dumb guy who read comic books.

It's easy these days to be cynical about classic novels. The term belongs to an age that still believed in self-improvement through reading the best that has been written. But I first got interested in reading because my mum told me about this wonderful classic called *The Catcher in the Rye*. Suddenly I found a friend, a voice saying all the things I wish I had said. From that moment on I realised that reading classic books would teach me to speak a language you could only learn from the printed page. And for that I'm grateful.

People often say that having to read classic novels at school put them off those books for life. I disagree. I doubt if I would have discovered the joys of D. H. Lawrence or Huxley if a teacher had not showed me how to read between the lines.

People tend to make too much of a fuss about classic novels – they are attacked for being elitist or celebrated for being absolutely essential. Classic novels are simply the works we want to pass on to the next generation of readers. And anyway, we talk about classic pop albums, classic films and classic sporting events, so why not classic novels?

Classic novels are important to read because such texts are the tickets that admit you into the great debates and conversations about literature. We need to talk about novels as much as we need to read them – classics are the ones that people will still be discussing long after anyone reading this will be dead.

What are your ten essential classic novels for the next 100 years?

My ten essential classic novels are as follows:

Remembrance of Things Past by Marcel Proust

The Brothers Karamazov by Fyodor Dostoevsky

The Trial by Franz Kafka

The Catcher in the Rye by J. D. Salinger

Nineteen Eighty-four by George Orwell

The Hobbit by J. R. R. Tolkien

Hangover Square by Patrick Hamilton

A Flag for Sunrise by Robert Stone

Sophie's Choice by William Styron

The Great Gatsby by F. Scott Fitzgerald

What are the books you believe should never have been called classics?

If you don't mind I'd rather not nominate ten books that should never be called classics.

COSMO LANDESMAN *is a well-known journalist and critic.*

David Lodge

What is your definition of a classic?
A classic novel is a novel that goes on being read by significant numbers of people long after the time of its original composition and publication. A major classic will also have the capacity to be read more than once by the same individual reader, yielding new meanings and pleasures on each re-reading.

I was not oppressed by the notion of the classic novel in childhood, nor turned off literature by being obliged to read classic novels at school. But like most children I tended towards light juvenile fiction, including comics, in my leisure hours.

Literary fiction is more often focused on the recent or distant past than on the future, but contemporary novelists who have shown an interest in speculating about the future include Julian Barnes and Michael Frayn.

Human nature will not change on 31 December 1999. The attributes of a great or even good novelist will be the same in the twenty-first century as they were in the twentieth: intelligence, good recall of what one has experienced or observed, a narrative imagination, and an ability to evoke a multiplicity of voices and discourses, spoken and written, that mediate reality, and to combine them into a personal style.

What are your ten essential classic novels for the next 100 years?

Tom Jones by Henry Fielding

Tristram Shandy by Laurence Sterne

Emma by Jane Austen

Jane Eyre by Charlotte Brontë

Bleak House by Charles Dickens

Middlemarch by George Eliot

The Ambassadors by Henry James

The Heart of Darkness by Joseph Conrad

Ulysses by James Joyce

Women in Love by D. H. Lawrence

If I had to teach a course on the English novel, with only ten set texts, these are the ones I would choose.

What are the books you believe should never have been called classics?

It is futile for an individual reader to say that any given book should never have been called a classic. The status of 'classic' is accorded to a book collectively, over time, by an entire culture. You may say you don't personally enjoy or admire such and such a classic, but that is a different matter. Research has shown that there is only room for a finite number of classics in the collective consciousness: old ones drop out as new ones are added to the canon. The novels of George Meredith might be cited as falling into the former category.

DAVID LODGE *is a writer and academic. His novels include* Small World, Nice Work *and* Paradise New, *and he has also written several works of literary criticism.*

Roger McGough

What is your definition of a classic?

To me 'classic' novels are novels that appear on the shelves in bookshops under 'Classics', and are invariably published in series clearly marked 'Classics'.

I disliked classic novels at school (up to the age of fifteen anyway, when I was lucky enough to fail Eng. Lit. at O-level and was not force-fed them again).

They were unattractively produced with thin (paper-thin?) paper and eye-scrunching print. I suffered *The Mayor of Casterbridge* at fourteen – far too young to appreciate it and the experience put me off Hardy for years. It was the poetry that led me back to him (as well as Julie Christie).

I shouldn't think any decent author is writing with an eye on the future. But, for me, the storytellers who love the poetic power of language will survive – Beryl Bainbridge, Vikram Seth, Sebastian Faulks, A. S. Byatt, Paul Theroux, Adam Thorpe, Salman Rushdie, Peter Ackroyd, Milan Kundera, Graham Greene.

What are your ten essential classic novels for the next 100 years?

I assume that any list of essential 'classics' would include such all-time greats as Dickens, Balzac, Tolstoy, Dostoevsky, Zola, D. H. Lawrence and Thomas Hardy, and so, acknowledging their 'classic' status, I venture to submit a list of more recent 'classics' (in no particular order):

The Catcher in the Rye by J. D. Salinger

Pale Fire by Vladimir Nabokov

A Portrait of the Artist as a Young Man by James Joyce

As I Walked Out One Midsummer Morning by Laurie Lee

Slaughterhouse 5 by Kurt Vonnegut

The Great Gatsby by F. Scott Fitzgerald

Earthly Powers by Anthony Burgess

I, Claudius by Robert Graves

One Hundred Years of Solitude by Gabriel Garcia Marquez

The Periodic Table by Primo Levi

What are the books you believe should never have been called classics?

For reasons given above I have read insufficient classics (as in the dog-eared, hand-me-down schoolboy variety) to differentiate.

ROGER MCGOUGH *has written numerous volumes of poetry for both adults and children, as well as plays and television programmes.*

Chris Meade

What is your definition of a classic?

When I was a teenager my girlfriend's family had a shelf of black Penguin classics, which I thought was the ultimate symbol of intellectual sophistication. I'm not sure my children's friends are so impressed by mine.

What are classic novels? They can be bought by the yard in leather to fill the shelves of Classic homes. They are cheap in paperback these days but the print is very small. They are all based on Andrew Davies screenplays. They have very downbeat blurbs on the back cover saying things like, 'Although this is far from being Henry James' finest novel . . .'

Real classics are the intimidating ones I haven't managed to read yet. The ones I've already enjoyed become simply Good Books, the best are treasure islands in my personal ocean of becoming. These are the books I mark decades of my life by and give to friends for Christmas, whether they want them or not.

What are your ten essential classic novels for the next 100 years?

Classicity became a phoney fragrance in the 1980's, a spray-on instant poshness applied alike to blue jeans, trainers, shopping malls, radio stations and albums of recycled pop. I'm not sure classic status is good for a novel, but here anyway are my nominations for 'Now That's What I Call The Most Classic Novels Ever':

War and Peace by Leo Tolstoy. A predictable choice but unavoidable.

Simply the best. A kind of fictional I Ching: open it at any page and find something to shed light on an aspect of your life. Makes Napoleon's invasion of Russia seem curiously relevant to planning the Annual General Meeting of the Poetry Society.

A Suitable Boy by Vikram Seth. Another epic literary soap opera to keep by the bedside and sip nightly like cocoa. The shoe-manufacturing suitor is one of the best literary descriptions of the business brain I've come across.

Nights at the Circus by Angela Carter. We (middle)named our daughter Fevvers, after the winged acrobat heroine. Just imagine what Carter might have written by now if she were still alive – but of course the trouble is we can't imagine.

Small World by David Lodge. Assuming that laughing doesn't go out of fashion in the twenty-hundreds, I believe this tale of ambitious, randy, globe-trotting academics will be painfully hilarious for the foreseeable future.

Stick by Elmore Leonard. I've been buying his books for years and am fed up he's become so popular that I can't introduce him to friends anymore. This, the first one I hit on, really is Classic Leonard: ex-con hero, two feisty women – one good, one bad – pursued by utter nutter. Oh yes.

À la Recherche du Temps Perdu by Marcel Proust. I've still not read it from beginning to end, but luxuriate in its sentences on a regular basis. *Ulysses* likewise. Books like these are what makes early retirement such an attractive option. Oh, and Dostoevsky.

Time's Arrow by Martin Amis. This rewind of our age is brilliantly realised and I think its surreal reversal of the Holocaust is incredibly shocking. I like it too because its special effects are only possible on the printed page.

Fugitive Pieces by Anne Michaels. Recent but destined to endure. A truly poetic novel, i.e. deeply moving and beautifully written, not poetic, meaning flowery, obscure and plotless.

One Hundred Years of Solitude by Gabriel Garcia Marquez. This trance of a book opened up thrilling new doors for imaginative literature, as centuries before did Cervantes's *Don Quixote*, Knight of the Sad Countenance, perhaps the first Magic Realist.

Middlemarch by George Eliot. Another predictable choice, but I didn't like it on telly because the best character didn't appear. If the post of God is vacant, I nominate George Eliot as the authorial voice I'd most like to be narrated by.

What are the books you believe should never have been called classics?

Crap new novels billed as 'destined to be classics of their kind', presumably classic crap novels. Erotic 'classics' by Anon that they sell on station bookstalls (which of course I never look at). Dickens. As a child I overdosed badly on his struggling orphans and wicked wards with ludicrous names and weird speech impediments.

But only schoolchildren, scholars and critics are forced to read books against their will and so get furious about ones they dislike. Everyday readers like me just put books down and start something else without having to analyse who is to blame for the breakdown between reader and writer. Call me a wimp, but I don't think slaggings and slatings stimulate good literature. Novelists should beware being lured into media slanging matches, which are deeply off-putting.

And finally, why, oh why no room for classic poetry? Well I would say that, wouldn't I, but for instance Ted Hughes published two works destined for instant classicisation before he so sadly departed, and while the last thing I'd want to do is encourage any more book-length poems about ex-loves, *Birthday Letters* and *Tales from Ovid* do prove that poets can write best-selling literary page-turners. 'Classic' sections in bookshops mingle poetry and prose and I'd like to see more of that in the bookshops of the future.

CHRIS MEADE *is the Director of The Poetry Society.*

Andrew Miller

What is your definition of a classic?

For me, the classic novels are those books which, year after year, I pull off the shelf, either to read in their entirety or to savour some much loved fragment. I do not consider myself to be particularly well read. I have never read Proust or *War and Peace*. Neither have I read all of Dickens's novels or Jane Austen's. The following list of 'classics' I wrote down on an Air France napkin while flying from San Francisco to Paris. On another day I might have written quite a different list but each of these novels is exceptional for its intelligence, ambition and passion; all we can reasonably ask for from any work of art.

What are your ten essential classic novels for the next 100 years?

Bleak House by Charles Dickens

Jane Eyre by Charlotte Brontë

Crime and Punishment by Fyodor Dostoevsky

Tess of the D'Urbervilles by Thomas Hardy

The Portrait of a Lady by Henry James

The Trial by Franz Kafka

A Portrait of the Artist as a Young Man by James Joyce

Lolita by Vladimir Nabokov

Memoirs of Hadrian by Marguerite Yourcenar

A Handful of Dust by Evelyn Waugh

I realise that the above is wildly euro-centric. It is not intended as anything other than a highly personal 'canon' of ten remarkable books. Had I been flying TWA or JAL, I am sure that favourites such as Faulkner or Bellow or Kawabata would have been on the napkin.

ANDREW MILLER *is the author of two novels,* Ingenious Pain *and* Casanova.

Adrian Mitchell

What is your definition of a classic?

A classic novel is a good old story which I'm trying to persuade you to read, you ignorant barbarian. As a child I loved most of the 'classics' which were read aloud to me, especially *Peter Rabbit, The Wind in the Willows, Huckleberry Finn* and Andrew Lang's *Tales of Troy and Greece*, but most especially *Treasure Island* in my father's warm Scottish accent.

Later, during a failed educational experiment called examinations, I was supposed to read *Silas Marner* but refused to because I thought it was a story about a miser. One of the best things a teacher can do is read aloud but only stories the teacher cares about. Turn your classroom into a theatre and give 'em your Dickens, your Brontë, your Kafka and your Pratchett. (So long as they don't have to write bloody essays about it afterwards.) Then give them a turn to read their favourites aloud.

The qualities a novel will need in the twenty-first century are: a story as wild as *The Odyssey*, language as rich as *King Lear* and Edward Lear, and a voice as individual as Paul Robeson, Betty Carter or Little Richard. Even then a readership will not be assured. Chances are that the readership will be wiped out as World War Three breaks out and the planet is burned to stone.

What are your ten essential classic novels for the next 100 years?

I decided to confine myself to novels published in Britain and

Ireland since 1900, which meant leaving out, among my top favourites, Fitzgerald's *The Great Gatsby*, Nathanael West's *Miss Lonelyhearts*, Vonnegut's *Cat's Cradle* and *Slaughterhouse Five* and Ursula Le Guin's *A Wizard of Earthsea*. My list is:

Jampot Smith by Jeremy Brooks. An amazing story of childhood in World War Two, by a very underestimated writer.

The True Heart by Sylvia Townsend Warner. Pure crystal.

Titus Groan by Mervyn Peake. (Plus *Gormenghast*, of course).

Nights at the Circus by Angela Carter. (Though some days I prefer her *Wise Children*.)

The Human Factor by Graham Greene. The great spy story.

The Magic City by E. Nesbit. Magical Realism is born.

Ulysses by James Joyce. You know.

Albert Angelo by B. S. Johnson. One of his great novels.

Jambo by Dave Ward. City life seen from underneath in a little-known illustrated masterpiece published by Impact Books.

Smallcreep's Day by Peter C. Brown. A super-realist story of life in a gigantic factory. A powerful prophecy.

Thank you for listening. Find them if you can and read them, aloud.

What are the books you believe should never have been called classics?

As for nominating ten books that I believe should never have been called classics, I'm happy to point to any five of Anthony Powell's *A Plod to the Music of Time* and any five Anthony Trollopes, because the very thought of them makes my wings itch.

ADRIAN MITCHELL *is a poet, playwright and children's author.*

Michael Moorcock

What is your definition of a classic?

I grew up reading anything I could get hold of. I read classics and I read trash. I read some trashy classics and some classical trash. George Bernard Shaw and Edgar Rice Burroughs. I had little formal schooling so didn't know I had to rank the books in any way at all. I learned that later, to my astonishment.

As someone who has published in pulps and literary magazines and has enjoyed a fair number of generic and literary prizes, I know that most contemporary opinion, including my own, has as much to do with fashion as taste. I know that a book published in a pulp format is ignored by literary critics and well reviewed when, under another title, it appears from a reputable publisher. One of my own earliest thrillers was done first by the Hank Janson firm and second, with a title change, by Hutchinson. Jack Trevor Story retitled his Sexton Blake stories and published them with Secker and Warburg. That's how relative things are, I think. However, I'm not sure relativism has much to do with what makes a classic.

A classic for me is something that sets a benchmark – something that probably hasn't been done quite that way before and gives us a fresh level of aspiration. Something which bears the stamp of an individual (known or not), is written in vivid, vital language and was probably thought a bit vulgar or too intense when it first came out. Shakespeare, Dickens, Zola, Tolstoy, Proust, Mann and Joyce (in *Ulysses*) have longevity and authority precisely because they are masters of pretty much all the elements we look for in good fiction –

eloquence, characteristic voice, memorable characterisation, absorbing narrative, a moral, observant eye, an ability to offer many stories in one story, an element of universality. These are the great classics.

Established classics, such as Austen's and Eliot's, brought in their own day a new voice, a new narrative method, a new sensibility to fiction. They remain alive precisely because of their inherent tensions, retaining the vitality always found in work where an innovative author is in unfamiliar territory, creating fresh language and finding new methods to describe experience for which the existing language and techniques are inadequate.

Although fashion had much to do with what was borrowed from Mudie's famous library, public taste pretty much determined what became a classic until sometime near the beginning of the twentieth century.

Suddenly the selection was taken from public hands and made a matter of university literary politics. Fiction became judged not so much by the authenticity of its voice and the authority of its language, but by how successfully it addressed middle-class sensibilities and concerns. I see the decline as beginning after the catholic founders of the two great English schools (Raleigh at Oxford, Quiller-Couch at Cambridge) lost authority to the politicking of F. R. Leavis (whose critical insights I greatly admire and whose tastes I generally share) and his followers, who brought a puritan narrowness to the discipline. As careers and to some extent fortunes came to depend on literary reputations being maintained, this involved all kinds of political selections and rejections and gave us the whole failed farce of Bloomsbury (which provided us with a couple of major writers and a lot of fairly uninteresting minor ones).

The effect of this sectarian authority was, of course, to exclude the vulgar, the lively and the eccentric in favour of a standard canon obeying certain well-defined rules. Generally speaking eccentric vulgarity lasts a lot longer than punctilious fashionability. An established body of opinion takes on the characteristics of a conservative orthodoxy which communicates its judgments to the anxious middle-class (for whom social agreement and approval is everything) so that minor work by Waugh is constantly reprinted and read while the great novels of John Cowper Powys, for instance, are hardly ever seen.

My own favourite nineteenth-century novelist, George Meredith, remains cruelly un-represented – with several of his best books out of print for fifty years – and will no doubt continue to be so while respectable critics repeat the opinions of their forebears and reinforce their prejudices (it's a great relief to the middle classes to be told what to exclude and, indeed, what to accept; the real function of our literary prizes). The fact that Meredith was often James's superior, in language, technique, story-telling, moral under-standing and sensibility, is nowadays known only to a few frustrated enthusiasts and those who take the trouble to seek out books like *The Amazing Marriage* in second-hand editions. For me there are a handful of minor classics from the same period which offer an understanding of the period impossible to find in more consciously literary work. These writers are sometimes associated with Gissing, but lack his despair. Arthur Morrison, W. Pett Ridge, Israel Zangwill, E. Nesbit and Leonard Merrick are among them. They provide a deep, authentic picture of the times and their London is neither a murky Dickensian swamp nor a spare Jamesian stage, but a real, working, ordinary place whose populations have concerns and daily lives very similar to our own. Useful perspective for those with millennial anxieties.

As you go through the twentieth century that divergence is magnified, I think. While the greatness and endurance of Conrad, Faulkner, Joyce and Woolf can't be in much doubt, most of the other anglophone writers selected for classic status don't really do very well from our scrutiny. Hemingway, under Pound's stern tutelage, imported some popular techniques and (unfortunately) sentiments into modern fiction, but I've always found it very difficult to perceive the likes of Evelyn Waugh and Graham Greene, enjoyable as they are, as classic writers. Academics, of course, feel relief at their conventions. I think the best work of E. M. Forster, Iris

Murdoch and Angus Wilson deserves a permanent place on the shelves but, however jolly and funny they can be, I'm surprised by the perception of the likes, say, of Barnes and the Amises as anything but writers of the moment. The commercial successes of such sentimentalists as Irvine Welsh aren't hard to understand – every generation produces its own versions.

Under-class fiction is only interesting to the middle-class reader if it seems to involve a 'problem'. Something which frightens or otherwise concerns them directly. To a middle-class reader who only understands the alienated and the dispossessed as an alarming problem, most lower-middle-class and working-class fiction is mysterious. Even middle-class fiction about the working class is mysterious. Like certain regional fiction, it's bought in larger numbers at times of economic uncertainty, when the mob seems to have moved a little further up the avenue (eg *The Ragged Trousered Philanthropists*). Writers with rather more authority than Waugh or Greene, but whose concerns were different, have disappeared almost completely from the public consciousness. They were never part of an academic canon. Neither did they address or aspire to be part of the dominant class.

I've seen this process of invisibility happen to some of our more recent writers, such as Gerald Kersh and Jack Trevor Story, both lower-middle-class prodigies. To eccentric geniuses like Edward Whitmore, even Firbank, and half a dozen others, all of whom deserve to have their best work available as enduring minor classics. I know how easy it is to disappear.

One of my favourite authors, who befriended me when I was young, was Mervyn Peake. In the mid-sixties, Peake's *Gormenghast* trilogy was saved from wretched obscurity by a decision, conspired at by myself, Langdon Jones (text editor) and Oliver Caldecott (editor-in-chief), with the help of Anthony Burgess, to make it a Penguin 'Modern Classic'. Until then, the original publisher had let the books go out of print and believed them to have no further market. They were actively resisting the restoration of a text which they themselves had butchered. The public had accepted Kingsley Amis's dismissive words, that the work was that of 'a bad fantasy writer of maverick status', and shown no interest. Since their republication they have rarely been out of print. Other fine writers haven't had the same chance.

Snobbery (exclusivity) and fashion continue to dominate contemporary taste. A hundred years ago a similar survey in *The English Illustrated Magazine* revealed that writers such as Walter Bagehot and Hall Caine were considered immortal, while James, Conrad and Wells didn't get a mention. Even by the 1920's a writer in *The Bookman* was wondering if George Eliot would last.

If Wells wrote presciently with an eye to the twentieth century, I suppose Philip K. Dick and Alfred Bester (now both deservedly Vintage classics) are the two who seem to have foreseen the textures, social conditions and concerns of the twenty-first century with the most success. I already feel that I'm living in one of their novels. But if it's a twenty-first-century sensibility we're talking about, I think that non-linear narratives are likely to address that most successfully. Imagine the range of choices and possibilities we will need to select from, almost continuously, if we wish to survive with any degree of personal satisfaction in an increasingly complex multiverse. Flexible, non-linear thinking is already best-suited for dealing with modern society. Interactive games, with several choices, prepare children for an increasingly changing world. Out of this culture will come our twenty-first-century electronically-savvy novelists.

We're already seeing experiments in online fiction and ultimately I think the novel as such will give way to increasingly sophisticated and coherent computer-delivered fictions, using everything the multimedia form can provide. The internet by its nature lends itself to an inclusive, humanistic and pluralistic overview and can be seen as a perfect marriage of science and art.

Interactive fiction, offering multiple story-lines, will be pretty familiar, I'd guess, within the next twenty years. It will be possible to carry as many narratives as one likes on winking moonbeams (lasers) whose capacities are almost limitless and which will be our chief means of communication.

The creative genius of the twenty-first century might well be some kind of renaissance all-rounder doing everything the novelist does, writing with eloquence, creating characters, telling stories, but also writing and performing the music, making the visuals, all with a unique perception which will inevitably produce a work of extraordinary coherence and effect. Intoxicated with these new instruments, inspired by them, as Shakespeare was with his, will she be the new millennium's Shakespeare? And set a whole new standard of aspiration to last for centuries? Imagine an all-encompassing movie stimulating every sense and a spectrum of emotions, supplying original psychological insights by a variety of means, engaging your absolute attention but characteristically produced by one person, an individual sensibility. That will be the first multi-media classic.

Meanwhile, as always, there will be a particular pleasure in reading. I don't expect the novel to die. I certainly hope it doesn't. I've made a fairly large investment in it.

What are your ten essential classic novels for the next 100 years?

I'd like to believe that the following ten twentieth-century classics will continue to be read for at least the next century:

Victory by Joseph Conrad (perfect, relentless plot, complex relation-ships)

No Laughing Matter by Angus Wilson (subtly different family chronicle)

The Heat of the Day by Elizabeth Bowen (totally gripping miniature)

Fowler's End by Gerald Kersh (funniest novel in English)

Gormenghast by Mervyn Peake (visionary, eloquent, larger-than-fiction characters, gripping plot)

Mercy by Andrea Dworkin (a moving, despairing, eloquent book)

One Last Embrace by Jack Trevor Story (an heroically funny fictional memoir)

Wise Children by Angela Carter (London hoofers look back – her best)

The Stars My Destination by Alfred Bester (visionary anarchist Dumas)

To the Lighthouse by Virginia Woolf (subtle shiftings of understanding)

What are the books you believe should never have been called classics?

And here's a few I'd gladly see the back of:

The Lord of the Rings by J. R. R. Tolkien (nursery porridge)

Lucky Jim by Kingsley Amis (creaking farce for croaking oldsters)

Narnia by C. S. Lewis (prozac-laced mush)

A Dance to the Music of Time by Anthony Powell (thin snobberies, literary muzak)

The Old Man and the Sea by Ernest Hemingway (macho tosh)

The House at Pooh Corner by A. A. Milne (syrupy honey)

Heart of Darkness by Joseph Conrad (numinous near-tosh)

Tender is the Night by F. Scott Fitzgerald (sentimental total tosh)

Who Killed Roger Ackroyd? by Agatha Christie (fat snobberies, generic muzak)

Under the Volcano by Malcolm Lowry (drunken tosh)

MICHAEL MOORCOCK *has written more than seventy novels in all genres – including the classic* Cornelius Chronicles, *the* Dancers at the End of Time *trilogy and the* Elric Saga.

Kate Mosse

What is your definition of a classic?

Classic – a Book with a Beard

Talking to a class of eight-year olds in south-east London once, I asked them if I looked like a writer. No, miss. No? Why's that then? You haven't got a beard, says the girl in front. You're not old, says her friend. And you've got nice shoes . . . Hmm. Bit depressing that. We've hit 1999 and yet the image of an author is still a shabby, pipe-smoking man in tweed. And their idea of a classic novel? Books you should have read, but haven't. Boring. Old-fashioned. Not relevant. Too long. So, there we have it. The definition of a classic as perceived by one class of Year 4 students, is simply, a book with a beard . . .

No, Seriously . . .

Sorry. I guess my own definition shifts, depending on my mood and how savage I'm feeling about the way in which reputations are constructed or propped up or manipulated by reviewers, profile writers and marketing departments with big budgets. When the wind's in a certain direction, the cynic in me would say that it's easy to force one book to outlive another. By spending money and calling in favours, it's not impossible to ensure that an author or novel is plastered everywhere – all the radio shows, all the telly book programmes with annoying titles, all the broadsheets' Lifestyle sections. You know what I mean. The triumph of strong-arm tactics and insider-dealing over talent.

In fairer mood, although I believe that filibustering tactics can keep one book in print longer than the next, I'm not convinced it results in anything more than a concentrated and glitzy shelf-life. Short-term success, sure, not long-term. We can all name bestsellers – *Captain Corelli's Mandolin*, for example – that were created by the buyers of fiction rather than (or in spite of) the purveyors of it. And we like it. Most of us like to think you can fool most of the people some of the time, blah, blah, but that you can't keep it up forever. The victory of the underdog. So, perhaps I'm being naive, but I too cling to the idea that a real classic cannot be 'made'. Not in that way, at least. That endurance and longevity is deserved. That it is the nature of a classic – the story, the characters, the atmosphere – that makes it distinct, that keeps it being read through generations. More than that, the way in which one particular novel, out of all those published at a given time, continues to influence writers that follow ten, twenty, even several hundred years later. Classics are distinct precisely because they exist out of time. Context is no object, experience or place no object, because the ideas and characters resonate long after the author is dead.

Of course, you can run into trouble with this idea of a literary fixed point of reference. I accept that a book's place in our collective consciousness sometimes owes more to the screen than to the page. We can all rattle off characters who, like Pirandello's, have escaped the confines of their story and now exist outside the restrictions of time and place of their original text: Mary Poppins, Frankenstein's Monster, James Bond, Scrooge, Casanova, Pollyanna, Mr Darcy even. All of them classics of a sort, but more honestly classics of popular culture rather than literature.

Hit or Miss?

But, assuming literary rather than popular reputation, let's think about if it's affection or status that matters most. What's it to be?

Personal favourites versus collective ones. Is a classic a novel you return to again and again, that informs and defines your own history? Or is it a book considered by the culture in which we live to be significant? Those that make us feel cultured and educated through the mere act of handing over our money, before we've even cracked the spine. When – if – we finish them, there is an automatic sense of having another piece of required reading under our belts. It's part of the deal. It's what we mean when we say someone is well-read and it has little to do with enjoyment, everything to do with superiority and being part of a club. For me, this club includes most of James Joyce, all of Marcel Proust, a hell of a lot of Dickens. Sorry. None of these do it for me. Actually, I could add Swift, Kundera and Rushdie to that list. I admire them, admire their achievements and their legitimate claim to be on any list of classics of the twentieth, nineteenth, eighteenth centuries . . . but not on mine.

Of course, the distinction between the personal and the collective classic doesn't always exist. Often, a favourite book is at one and the same time a novel considered 'great' by many people too (*Pride and Prejudice* and *Frankenstein* appear both above and below). But not necessarily and I think there's far too much literary bullying, too little standing up for taste. Any worthwhile list must be informed by individual preference rather than made up of titles chosen for the express purpose of impressing some imagined critic. Why should we care if our choices don't measure up? If we are judged to be too popular, too clichéd, too commercial . . . In any case, if we don't tell the truth, for fear of what we think it might reveal about us, then what about everybody else? If we're lying, then why shouldn't we assume everyone else is lying too? That everyone's list is artificially designed to make them look clever? Maybe, just maybe, nobody really likes Proust . . .

What are your ten essential classic novels for the next 100 years?

And the result is . . . in no particular order.

So, shooting from the heart rather than the hip, here're my

classics. Favourites, all of them. All books that mean something to me. I make no claim for any of them other than that.

Wuthering Heights by Emily Brontë

The Women's Room by Marilyn French

Nostromo by Joseph Conrad

Frankenstein by Mary Shelley

The Lion, the Witch and the Wardrobe by C. S. Lewis

The Lord of the Rings by J. R. R. Tolkien

Paradise Lost by John Milton (yes, I know it isn't, strictly speaking, a novel, but come on . . .)

The Woman in White by Wilkie Collins

The Mill on the Floss by George Eliot

Have the Men Had Enough? by Margaret Forster

The Pale Horse by Agatha Christie

The End of the Affair by Graham Greene

A Severed Head by Iris Murdoch

Pride and Prejudice by Jane Austen

Too many for a Top Ten, I appreciate. Pretty predictable, accessible, few surprises and nothing much from the very recent past, although that's probably just the nature of the beast. Novels published in the past ten years or so, say, simply haven't had time to settle down inside us yet. It's obvious that these pre-millennial 'Best of . . .' lists are actually less about taste and more about time. Both our perceived lack of it – how hard it is to keep up and keep reading given work, children, responsibility, traffic jams, whatever – and the nature of it. We're too close. Years must pass before we can know what we value. How many years depends on us, both individually and severally. Posterity's not all it's cracked up to be. It depends on what happens, how we develop and where we end up. Mind you, it's enough to give anyone writing now pause for thought . . .

KATE MOSSE *is the co-founder of the Orange Prize for Fiction and the author of two novels,* Eskimo Kissing *and* Crucifix Lane.

Alistair Niven

What is your definition of a classic?

The problem with the word 'classic' is the same as with the word 'literature'. These are terms readily understood, admired and even loved by those who are in the professions of books and learning. In this age of political correctness, however, they smack of the most dreaded charge of all, namely that of elitism. To suggest that one thing is actually better than another is these days considered politically unacceptable. Never mind the fact that every time we name a child, choose some clothes in a shop, pass comment on a television celebrity, decide where we are going to have our holiday, or visit a library, we are making a choice based on our understanding of quality and pleasure. If we label an activity with a word that seems to carry with it even a whiff of superiority, then we have committed a crime against humanity. For this reason, the word and even the concept of the 'classic novel' is barely acceptable and hardly understood by anyone under forty. 'It's a classic' is as likely to be said about a song recorded a few years ago by Nirvana or about a stylish new breed of car as it is about a nineteenth-century novel or a seventeenth-century play. I'm inclined, therefore, to recommend that we only use it in the most literal way: when we are referring to works by authors who are consciously echoing classicism as it can be defined in an Augustan or Periclean way. For the rest, let us move on and think in terms of 'favourite' or 'admirable' books which we would happily recommend to others as works of instruction or entertainment, the Scylla and Charybdis of all writing over the aeons.

I had the great good fortune to be encouraged by parents who did not mind that I read, providing I read something. If I was caught with Dan Dare under the bedclothes they were perfectly happy. Sometimes I picked up a light romance which my mother was reading, at other times I chose one of my father's books of famous trials, with which, looking back on it, he was worryingly obsessed. I remember when once I was ill in bed making myself sick with laughter as I read one of Richmal Crompton's *William* stories and today when I hear Martin Jarvis reading the same material, I do not wonder why. If ever there was English prose which deserved the word 'classic', it is here in these wonderfully funny and elegant tales of mischief and mayhem.

I was a pupil at Dulwich College, where P. G. Wodehouse and Raymond Chandler had also been once upon a time. There were other writers, too, with Dulwich associations, among them Dennis Wheatley. Every day on my way to school I would pass a pretty little house called Pickwick Cottage and it was said to be where Charles Dickens had anticipated Mr Pickwick spending his retirement days. Because I walked to school, I rarely read on buses or trains at that time, as I do now. I did, however, concoct endless stories of my own. They usually involved me being victorious in some great battle with malign forces, more Wheatley than Wodehouse. In my class for several years I sat next to Michael Ondaatje, who was not especially good at English, which I was said to be. Life can be mortifying. I was dimly aware of a youngster called Graham Swift. Both went on to write novels which by any definition are modern classics.

At the school itself I had inspired English teachers who encouraged me to read in the same spirit as my parents. They liked me to explore out-of-the-way authors and to express personal opinions in essays. In some ways I found going to Cambridge University as the next stage rather stultifying by comparison. When, for example, I wanted to work on the poetry of Hugh MacDiarmid, I found no one in the University who could supervise on him as he was clearly dismissed as a lightweight and unimportant. I think it was this penchant for writers who were slightly out of the main frame which

led me into Commonwealth and post-colonial writing, which became
the kernel of my academic work in ensuing years. There I could see in
writers such as Chinua Achebe, Mulk Raj Anand, Wilson Harris and
Patrick White the modern classic novel being born almost before my
eyes. I discovered a generation of Indian writers who had been largely
forgotten here in Britain and new possibilities for English-language
prose in the hands of Caribbean and Antipodean novelists. It was an
exciting discovery repeated almost every time I took a new book off
the shelves in the years I was working on my doctorate or teaching
courses in this newly forged area.

It is in the writings of so many novelists who were once regarded as
marginal but who have appropriated the centre of our attention that
the future possibilities for fiction lie. I have no truck with those who
predict the death of the novel. Neither in quantity nor quality is there
a flicker of evidence to support such pessimism, and the challenges of
new technology will help to distribute fiction rather than serve to
crush it. For the foreseeable future the interesting novelists are likely
to balance ardent internationalism with a knowledgeable sense of
their own locality. It is making sense out of this paradox which
interests me in the work of Salman Rushdie and so many other contemporary novelists. Humankind is on the move in endless sweeps of
migration and resettlement. Fixed opinions no longer stand up to
close examination. We are light years away from the omniscient self-
confidence of so many nineteenth-century so-called classic English
novelists. But displacement and uncertainty are energising processes
and I look with excitement and relish to the fiction which will emerge
in the next generation or so. Of course we shall see acres of post-
bonkbuster writing, but I think we shall also see at the core of modern
fiction new interfusions of languages, cross-referring between
English and other tongues, as well as a cultural mix which will
constantly question our assumptions and extend our horizons.

What are your ten essential classic novels for the next 100 years?

You asked me to nominate ten essential classic novels for the next

100 years. Everyone will name *Middlemarch* and Jane Austen but I hope we shall in a century from now still be reading *Jane Eyre* by Charlotte Brontë, *Jude the Obscure* by Thomas Hardy, *Sons and Lovers* by D. H. Lawrence and almost anything by Dickens. These are obvious choices, but from recent writing I believe the greatest novels are *Arrow of God* by Chinua Achebe, almost anything by R. K. Narayan, *A House for Mr Biswas* by V. S. Naipaul, and *Stone Angel* by Margaret Laurence. I think there are Scottish novels which deserve to be read 100 years from now, among them *The Silver Darlings* by Neil Gunn and *Magnus* by George Mackay Brown. Golding's *Lord of the Flies* will stand up to the test of time because it is such a simple allegory. I hope that some fairly obscure continental novels such as *Axel* by Bo Carpelan from Finland will be read not only in their own countries but in translation. I think that the best of Muriel Spark will always be read. I hope that we shall not have lost the ability to discover, as Virago did for my generation, lost writers whose reputations were neglected in the proceeding 100 years or whose work was never really accorded the recognition it deserved at the time it was published.

What are the books you believe should never have been called classics?

As for nominating books which should never have been called classics, I will stick my neck out and name *Vanity Fair* as the most overrated English novel. Its selection at the 1997 Cheltenham Literature Festival as the Booker Prize of 1848, when up against *Jane Eyre*, *Wuthering Heights* and *Dombey and Son*, astonished me. It is overlong, mean spirited and not very funny. I could name other so-called classics I have not much enjoyed, but what's the point? There are so many more that make one glad to be alive: *Tom Jones, Persuasion, Villette, Tess of the D'Urbervilles, Kim, The House with Green Shutters*. We don't have to label them 'classics' to know they are captivating stories in the characters of which we partly find our own.

ALASTAIR NIVEN *is Literature Director of the British Council.*

Lawrence Norfolk

What is your definition of a classic?

A classic should provide trust funds for one's grandchildren, be acclaimed by all and sundry, and elevate its author to the status of a god. A classic is a book that everyone believes is good, everywhere and always.

But such books are created by their readers rather than their writers. The status is conferred and the security of the judgment depends upon those readers' numbers and their historical spread. Above all, a classic must last. Our increasing geographical homogeneity makes it easier for a book to be all things to all men, but our ever-increasing temporal acceleration nixes any guarantee that today's classic will also be tomorrow's. The historical wave is the one to ride.

What are your ten essential classic novels for the next 100 years?

The next millennium could bring almost anything. Its classics will be the books that can be re-read in the light of those events, so picking them demands some prophesying, which is a fairly shoddy foundation, but perhaps good enough for literary criticism.

I think China and Africa will either descend into some godawful chaos or emerge as the new powerhouses. Whichever, their literary chroniclers will need godfathers, so Chinua Achebe's *Things Fall Apart*. I'm sure the Great Chinese Novel has been written, and stashed until a change in the political climate allows its publication.

Urbanisation seems unstoppable: Thomas Pynchon for Poet-in-Chief of our industrialised and city-bound lives, and *Gravity's Rainbow* as his prime text. Faulkner's *Absalom, Absalom!* for the ruralist dissenters.

I don't know what the next millennium will prove to contain, but I'm sure it will be complex and there'll be a lot of it. The form of the novel seems quite unstable at the moment. I see a fork in the tradition where compendious, multi-layered, allusive books could peel away from a more conservative line of humanistic testaments. Musil's *The Man Without Qualities* might supply the requisite open-ended model for the former stream, and Beckett's *Watt* the same for the latter. I think if the two could be synthesised Proust would already have done it, but *À la Recherche du Temps Perdu* is at the very limit of what is possible within the genre of the novel and marks an end rather than a beginning. Joyce's *Finnegans Wake* likewise.

The grim comedy of our various ethnicities and their discontents looks set to continue. I would pick Louis de Bernières as their likely laureate, perhaps his next book, or perhaps the *oeuvre* as a whole. Salman Rushdie has as good a claim; *Shame* over *Midnight's Children*, for myself.

Don DeLillo is the most prescient writer working today and *The Names* has a firm grip on what it means to be in transit, and in transition come to that. His novel *Ratner's Star* is more or less unreadable but the syzygy between literary art and science is clearly getting more important by the day. Antonia Byatt's *Collected Shorter Fiction* (whenever she gets around to actually collecting it) for the link to Darwinism and, at the other end of the spectrum, David Foster Wallace's *Infinite Jest* for the techno bits and bobs, and how to deal with them. Finally, two novels which I include on the twin grounds of sheer excellence and undeserved obscurity: Andrei Bely's *Petersburg* and Alejo Carpentier's *Explosion in a Cathedral*, which its original readers know as *El Siglo de las Luces*.

What are the books you believe should never have been called classics?

I feel unqualified to tear the badges of rank from the chests of my fellow-authors, but I suppose there are so-called 'classics' which are really rather ordinary. A lot of Gide's work looks very dated now – *The Counterfeiters* in particular – and I've never really seen the necessity of Trollope. I prefer to think of novels which really should have been classics but are not: Harold Brodkey's *The Runaway Soul* (hacked out of a filing cabinet of manuscripts with a necessarily brutal editorial axe), J. D. Salinger's Glass family chronicle (either waiting to be similarly hacked-out, or non-existent) and the novel which Thomas Pynchon should have been writing instead of wasting twenty years on *Mason and Dixon*.

Universality and longevity are tough artistic hurdles, and there's a rather obvious hermeneutic problem as to where one might stand to witness their being cleared. It's hard to be everywhere and always. Strictly speaking, 'classics' do not, have not, and probably cannot ever exist.

The catch is in that 'probably'. The real value of 'a classic' is that it remains a possibility, even if a vanishingly small one. One would like to write one and, as you begin the long work of producing a novel, it is just possible in that first flush of optimism to believe that you will. The idea of a classic is helpful, in a megalomaniacal way. Of course, after you've finished your novel and realised that it's not a classic, gloom descends. This is personally unfortunate, but megalomania and gloom are appropriate states of mind for a novelist.

One is left with Almost-Classics: books which almost everyone believes are good, almost everywhere, almost always. I suppose Shakespeare's works qualify, and perhaps *The Iliad*. Novels tend to become too diffuse when they reach after universality. I don't think my own books will be seen as classics, but that's OK. My grand-children can shift for themselves.

LAWRENCE NORFOLK *is the author of two novels,* Lemprière's Dictionary *and* The Pope's Rhinoceros.

Tom Paulin

What is your definition of a classic?

A classic novel is one which over several generations has been praised and admired by both general readers and literary critics. It is often studied and is viewed as a significant part of the literary canon. Classics are important to our sense of an enduring and significant culture, and they often feel part of our lives in the way that certain relatives and friends, as well as certain places, do. As a schoolchild, I found that some of Dickens's novels – *Oliver Twist, David Copperfield, Great Expectations* – seemed part of the fabric of the gloomy Victorian building that was and remains Rosetta Primary School. In my early years there I thought the headmaster looked like Charles Dickens. I think Douglas Coupland, author of the brilliant post-modernist novel *Girlfriend in a Coma,* is writing with an eye on the twenty-first century. The qualities a novel will need for the twenty-first century are wit and a rejection of a monolingual, monocultural outlook. Such novels should aim to be post-nationalist.

What are your ten essential classic novels for the next 100 years?

Robinson Crusoe. The novel in English begins with Defoe. A prose version of *Paradise Lost,* it is one of the great imaginative achievements of English Puritanism.

Gulliver's Travels. Swift's satire mocks Defoe's humourless, dogged practicality, and is the first anti-colonial novel in English.

Clarissa by Samuel Richardson. There are two great epic novels in the English language – *Ulysses* and Richardson's neglected master-piece. This is a tragic vision of English history.

Tristram Shandy by Laurence Sterne. Sterne's novel is one of the funniest, most playful classics in the language. His Irish upbringing made him subvert various English certainties.

Emma by Jane Austen. Austen's novel is both a subtle psychological study of a young girl growing up and a clever political fiction.

Charles Dickens's *Great Expectations* is a brilliant parable of upward mobility launched at a highly self-satisfied society. It is viciously critical of mid-Victorian society, and is subversive, egalitarian and republican in its attitude to the class system.

Vanity Fair. Thackeray, like Marx in *The Communist Manifesto*, which was also published in 1848, offers an ironic hymn to capitalism in this wild, volatile and hilarious novel.

Moby Dick by Herman Melville. This is the great American novel, a gigantic epic which offers a prophetic vision of the destiny of the Republic of the United States.

Ulysses. Joyce's novel is arguably the last great novel in English. A comic masterpiece and a classical monument, it looks forward to a peaceful united Ireland, The New Bloomusalem.

Huckleberry Finn. Twain's masterpiece tells some stretchers like nobody else can.

What are the books you believe should never have been called classics?

Tom Jones by Henry Fielding. Good-hearted but tedious. Mono-tonous eighteenth-century prose.

Waverley. Scott's style, as Hazlitt observed, is desultory, vacillating and annoying.

The Portrait of a Lady. James's novel is a psychological melodrama which groups a series of flatly-realised characters round the central character, Isabel Archer.

Jude the Obscure by Thomas Hardy. A sour and misogynistic novel much overrated by sentimental radicals.

The Rainbow. Lawrence's repetitive prose flounders and is often tacky and repellent.

Women in Love by D. H. Lawrence. Belongs with a lot of daft ideas to the 1960's when the tedious film was made.

Howard's End. Forster's schematic novel is so obviously about business versus art.

To the Lighthouse. Woolf's snobbishly sensitive prose has many admirers for reasons which continue to escape me.

Lucky Jim. For some reason large numbers of the British reading public think Amis is the reincarnation of Evelyn Waugh. A beery, insular, racist philistine in my view. In one novel – *Jake's Thing* – he refers to 'an O'Casey peasant'. Ain't no such thing.

TOM PAULIN *is a lecturer, poet, broadcaster and writer. His latest book is* The Day-Star of Liberty: William Hazlitt's Radical Style.

Tim Pears

What is your definition of a classic?

A classic novel means different things to different people. To a
middle-aged person like myself it induces a queasy squib of guilt that
one hasn't read the novel in question, really ought to one day, and
never will; to a schoolchild it's a tedious chore in English lessons; to
a youth, a male one anyway, it's one of the categories of books to be
avoided. Of course, for most young men all categories of books are
to be avoided. Reading novels is something women do.

I had an English teacher who achieved the notable feat of having
my O-level class study *Twelfth Night* and putting us off Shakespeare
for years afterwards. Harold Bloom, bombastic defender of the
Western Canon, argues that to quarrel on behalf of aesthetic value is
always a blunder, which is true, and fine for a university lecturer to
say. The question is, how best to offer children the riches of our
literary inheritance?

An Anglican priest, my father read voraciously and shared his
discoveries through advocacy and argument over the dinner tale.
When my sisters and I were small he used to read a chapter of a
classic each night, then retell it to us the next evening: James
Fenimore Cooper, Charles Dickens. Books were a part of life –
Richmal Crompton's *Just William* series, Geoffrey Household's *Rogue
Male*, P. G. Wodehouse – until I was put off them at school. My
father's study remained a sanctuary, however, and I was saved by his
being something of a Russophile: Tolstoy, Dostoevsky, Gogol,
Goncharov – the nineteenth-century canon – seemed disconnected

to the Eng. Lit. books we were forced to study, and so I entered the
domain of Tsarist Russia. It colonised my imaginative landscape,
became a dream world, this society on both the torpid and hysterical
brink of cataclysm, thick with moral question and consequence,
ideal reading for a teenager.

Browsing: a beautiful word. The best thing we can offer the next
generation is places conducive to browsing. Feed children on folk
tales and fairy stories, introduce them to the King James Bible,
Homer, Ovid (Rex Warner's *Stories of the Greeks*), Shakespeare,
without which most of western literature loses its allusive texture.
Add an abridged Mahabharata and the Koran. Teach them Latin
and Greek, obviously. And then let them discover for themselves,
giving over half of school English lessons to silent reading sessions,
in which children can read what they want.

The notion of classics, of a canon, is vital as a storehouse of the
richest jewels of civilisation. But the dissemination of those riches is
what's important. A tiny percentage of the population could read
when *The Pilgrim's Progress* was written, compared with today's mass
literacy: tremendous, except that what we have is a standard of
education such that most people can now cope with the *Sun*. This is
the challenge. To open a child's cultural horizons beyond that of
their parents and peers, over and above odd extraordinary teachers
who galvanise receptive pupils. Does technology offer hope of
disseminating art, or is the next generation condemned to moronic
games?

Signs are hopeful. Modern bookshops are more welcoming now
than they've ever been; public libraries remain the most precious
asset, as long as they have the means of incorporating new
technology.

It's the end of the twentieth century and we're re-entering an odd
reflection of the nineteenth, in so many ways (in this two-nation –
or twenty-nation – Britain). The Internet promises participation.
People communicating with each other, organising reading groups,
writing groups, a vast new homespun literature, aesthetically mediocre no doubt but creative self-expression nonetheless. Victorians

sang around the piano in the parlour but they didn't imagine they were great musicians; and yet they valued, appreciated Schumann and Brahms. Didn't they?

What is a classic? A classic is what we ('we'? I mean 'they') agree to call a classic. It's what remains in print. Or: a classic in our own language is a book impossible to read without notes. A classic from another language remains modern, dated only by the available translation. (At least a novel, unlike poetry, can be translated in the first place.) One suspects we're entering a digital age when Harold Bloom's literary academy, having been battered by self-interest groups, will give way to the largest one of all: readers.

Do bookworms read Chaucer for pleasure? Rarely. People study Chaucer because they are paid to, or because (students lacking grants) they have paid to. Literature is a sect of the religion which is art, and its sacred texts become more arcane every year. Our scholars will guard the treasures until translators revitalise them for successive generations. This means the loss of literature that has been beached from language an educated person understands. But, after all, we can't predict how language will change, any more than we can humour.

Is this important? Shakespeare remains central to our canon, yet when we see, say, *As You Like It*, we have to endure long stretches of fools' wordplay which is neither clever nor funny any more.

What are your ten essential classic novels for the next 100 years?

I began to compile a list that included recent novels by extra-ordinary carvers of language, like Michael Ondaatje's *The English Patient*, a scrupulous layering of fragile words into a tough fabric of meaning; Ann Michaels's *Fugitive Pieces*, in which subject, language and form were born and grew together; *Debatable Land* by Candia McWilliam, whose sentences are made of thick pigment, every page like a Soutine painting.

I realise that, neither teacher nor academic, one should share less admiration than enthusiasm, and books I love most tend to create whole worlds and teem with characters, stories, humour, ideas; sprawling, messy and profligate. (I see my taste has changed, from the austerity demanded as a youth, perhaps; from Tarkovsky to Paradjanov.) Which applies to most, though hardly all, of the following:

One Hundred Years Of Solitude by Gabriel Garcia Marquez

Invisible Cities by Italo Calvino

A Farewell to Arms by Ernest Hemingway

The House of the Spirits by Isabel Allende

Catch-22 by Joseph Heller

The Life and Times of Michael K by J. M. Coetzee

The Cider House Rules by John Irving

The Satanic Verses by Salman Rushdie

Moon Palace by Paul Auster

The War of Don Emmanuel's Nether Parts by Louis de Bernières

What are the books you believe should never have been called classics?

I believe John Irving said in an interview that one of the benefits of becoming an adult is that you don't have to finish a book you're not enjoying. It's a basic human right, which ought perhaps to be extended to children. So, I refuse to nominate books as undeserving of being called classics; if someone passionately advocates their being read, they are classic. As long as that person doesn't force other people to finish them.

Lastly, why read a (classic) novel? Harold Bloom claimed that, 'Reading deeply in the Canon will not make one a better or a worse person, a more useful or a more harmful citizen. The mind's dialogue with itself is not primarily a social reality. All that the Western Canon can bring one is the proper use of one's own solitude, that solitude whose final form is one's confrontation with one's own mortality.'

George Eliot, on the other hand, wrote, 'The only effect I ardently long to produce by my writings is that those who read them should be better able to imagine and to feel the pains and joys of those who differ from themselves in everything but the broad fact of being struggling, erring human creatures.'

I used to believe in the former, hermetic, magical, sacred view of art; I now tend to the latter, broader allegiance to society. But they're both right, of course, and will always be necessary.

TIM PEARS *is the author of two novels,* In the Place of Fallen Leaves *and* In a Land of Plenty.

Christopher Priest

What is your definition of a classic?

It seems to me that to become a 'classic' a book has to do one of two things. It should enjoy overwhelming popular support (crossing at least one generation) which leads eventually to critical appreciation, or it should attract a huge amount of critical or scholarly attention that sustains it while popular interest grows. The work of Charles Dickens is an example of the first, that of James Joyce the second. This is why best-selling novels usually fail to become classics (they aren't sufficiently interesting beyond their temporary appeal), and for the opposite reason why many critical successes eventually fall by the wayside. Popular acceptance is the key.

What are your ten essential classic novels for the next 100 years?

Ten classic works of twentieth-century fiction in alphabetical order by author (I decided to confine my list to twentieth-century fiction only).

Lucky Jim by Kingsley Amis. Everything that an Amis novel came to represent is here in his first: the unique take on middle-class England, the bad attitude, the wicked mimicry, the boozing, the practical jokes. I always felt that Kingsley Amis was a writer you should read all of, finding that the humour, the viewpoint, etc., would grow on you as you went along. I liked most of his novels, *Lucky Jim* no more than many of them, but it is probably the one everyone has heard of and read, so it fulfils the brief.

The Voices of Time by J. G. Ballard.[1] I can't imagine a list of potentially classic twentieth-century fiction without Ballard, when as a young and almost unknown writer, selling to obscure science fiction magazines, he was at his most innovative, mysterious and eloquent. *The Voices of Time* contains a selection of eight stories from that rich period before the novels, and represents the best, if not the best-known, of this unusual and intriguing writer.

The Magus by John Fowles. Fowles's masterpiece, a key novel of the twentieth century, whose influence has spread far and wide, not only with other writers but also with film-makers. It seems to appeal primarily to younger people, which might be one of the reasons it remains out of general critical favour, a novel some people seem reluctant to admire. Later attempts by the same author at similar themes – which Fowles once called the Game of God – tend to cast an unattractive backward light over *The Magus.* In this novel, his first-written but not his first-published, Fowles made the theme not only plausible and attractive but also universal. *The Magus* is a fascinating blend of psychological thriller, sexual comedy, philosophical discourse. I prefer the original of 1966 to the revised version eleven years later, because its lack of self-consciousness gives it an exhilarating freshness.

Dubliners by James Joyce. The finest short fiction of the twentieth century. In *The Dead* we have the greatest single short story of all.

Pet Sematary by Stephen King. King's novels are examples of those with a huge popular constituency, but for which critical acceptance is yet to come. I believe he is the Dickens of the twentieth century. King may well have written better novels than *Pet Sematary,* but he has published a huge number of books (many of them immensely long) and I have managed to read only a few of them. *Pet Sematary* is my own favourite of his. It's an extraordinary novel: it exerts a tremendous narrative hold over the reader, the world it depicts is all too realistic and understandable and the author employs several structural devices that I found daring, thrilling and impressive. I thought the 'horror' aspect of the novel was ironically the weakest part, but the true quality of the novel is the depiction of the believable characters involved in a fantastic experience. Writing in a flowing, natural style, King's easy familiarity with popular culture – junk food, TV signature tunes, children's games and so on – gives his work a compulsive immediacy that is unequalled.

The Painted Bird by Jerzy Kosinski. Any reckoning of twentieth-century literature should include novels of World War Two. *The Painted Bird* is one of the most unusual and effective WW2 novels I have read: a book so truly shocking that sometimes it is almost impossible to keep reading. The novel is a microcosm of human suffering, written in disjointed, alienating language, describing events that are horrific almost beyond comprehension. (It fulfils neither of my definitions of a classic, having come and gone and apparently left almost no trace – but maybe it will be rediscovered.)

The House at Pooh Corner by A. A. Milne. The earlier Pooh collection, *Winnie-the-Pooh*, has a less certain voice, the reader being addressed directly but intermittently. This second book is a masterpiece both of children's literature and literature itself: funny, subtle and subversive, with as many pleasures for adults as for children. I have always been moved by the end of *The House at Pooh Corner*, it's clearly a summation of the loss of childhood but on a more subtle level it's a release from childhood into growing up.

Nineteen Eighty-four by George Orwell. I believe that Orwell's great literary contribution is his non-fiction, but since we are confined here to fiction then it has to be *Nineteen Eighty-four*. It is of course a metaphorical portrait of Britain in the late 1940's, seen as a BBC-manipulated Stalinist state. If it weren't for the innovative use of language and the sophisticated understanding of the cynical methods of tyrannical government, the book would have had its day long ago. As it is, *Nineteen Eighty-four* is one of those novels that goes on being true and relevant.

Pavane by Keith Roberts. Anthony Burgess called *Pavane* 'fiction of hypothesis'; in this case the postulate is that Queen Elizabeth was assassinated in 1588, the Spanish swept in and England was restored to the Catholic Church. The novel itself is set in Dorset in the present day (the 1960's, in fact, when Roberts wrote the book) and depicts a world of scientific and technological suppression. The monasteries are custodians of many forbidden secrets: printing, radio, even the internal combustion engine. The novel is written in colourful, resonant language, it's crammed with intriguing details and feelings and is told with a wonderful sense of oddness and conviction. (There is a glancing, thinly disguised reference to *Pavane* in Kingsley Amis's novel *The Alteration* . . . I believe Keith Roberts feels that Amis pinched the idea from him.)

Loitering with Intent by Muriel Spark. I think Muriel Spark should become a classic author, with no one title singled out, but since I have to choose a title this one is it. I love Spark's attitude: a dry, matter-of-fact style, laced with witty asides and straight-faced observations. *Loitering with Intent* is probably less well known than some of her other titles, but she was at the height of her powers when she wrote it and many of her familiar subjects are targeted here.

What are the books you believe should never have been called classics?

On the Road by Jack Kerouac. When you hear the title for the first time, or someone tells you what it's about, *On the Road* seems to unfold wonderfully about you with seductive images of western highways and big skies and wild nights. The reality of the book is much less than this: *On the Road* is a banal and often incoherent narrative by someone who admires all the wrong things. Whenever I've tried to read more of it the book makes me think I'm trapped.

Lord of the Flies by William Golding. I always have to remind myself it was a first novel, so one shouldn't expect too much. It has nonetheless acquired classic status, and is normally approached with a reverence I find incomprehensible. While clearly allegorical in nature, the method of *Lord of the Flies* is so transparent that you begin to test the allegory rather than the novel as a work of fiction. When you do, you find that the allegory is tiresome and inconsistent, and that the author fudges his way through much of it.

More generally: anything by Virginia Woolf, Martin Amis, Jeanette Winterson, any of the James Bond novels of Ian Fleming, any of the thrillers by Dick Francis . . . I have seen all of these at one time or another accorded the status of 'classic', and they are all over-rated.

[1] *The Voices of Time* was originally published by Victor Gollancz in 1963 under the title *The Four-dimensional Nightmare*. It was reissued as *The Voices of Time* in 1984 (with a small variation in contents).

CHRISTOPHER PRIEST *is the author of many novels, including* The Prestige, The Glamour *and* The Extremes.

Stuart Proffitt

What is your definition of a classic?

A 'classic' is simply a book whose value has been recognised and has endured through time. 'Classics' might not be those books written in the past which we now think *most* important, valuable or interesting – but as long as it is still thought they have *some* importance, value, interest, they achieve that status. Recognition is important: a book may be a masterpiece, but if no one knows it or recognises it, it cannot be a classic. Johnson says, 'That book which the reader throws away is good in vain.' Endurance is important: a book must have been recognised by several generations of readers. (Claims for 'instant classics' are therefore only instantly tautologous.) These – value, recognition and endurance – are the essential qualities.

Identifying books which are either thought of as classics and shouldn't be, or aren't and should be, is a tricky business because, by my definition, millions of readers have been sifting the world's literature for a very long time removing such anomalies. But I have to admit that I cannot see why *Don Quixote*, for example, is still thought such a classic, almost an archetypal classic: perhaps it is because the *idea* of the book is so attractive that no one bothers to read it and discover how long and very, very boring it really is. Instead, now, classic status please for a book just admitted for the first time to Penguin Classics – *The Compleet Molesworth*.

Trying to identify books published very recently which will be thought classics in a hundred years time is much more fun, and much more dangerous. Books that break moulds often become classics because they are landmarks. So, for linguistic inventiveness and because they so convey the sense of our time, the best of Martin Amis's books will be there. So will Saul Bellow's – titanic novels in any age. So will those which, on their own terms, achieve some kind of perfection – those of William Trevor and Penelope Fitzgerald. So many others probably should, but because of the way the historical winnowing process works, probably won't. (Look back to what was published and read in the nineteenth century and see how little of it is still read today.) But what could we hope will survive to our great grandchildren more than *The Blue Flower*?

STUART PROFFITT *is Publishing Director for The Penguin Press.*

Philip Ridley

In true William Burroughs spirit ('When they give you lined paper, write the other way') I've ignored what I was asked to do. Why? Well, I have no idea what a classic is. I don't care. I'm looking at most of the critical 'Best of the Century' lists with a cast-of-the-*Nostromo*-seeing-the-chest-burster-for-the-first-time expression on my face. I can't believe what I'm seeing! It's just too horrific! So . . . here is my list of one hundred things that are just part of my life. If you were making a replicant of me (*à la Blade Runner*) these should be the first things filed into my memory chips (along with what Terry Jonson and I did to that dead cat when we were six – but that's another story).

1. *The X-Men* by Stan Lee (comic). As a child I was chronically sick with asthma. Sometimes for months at a time. The Marvel Universe kept me company: The Fantastic Four, Iron Man, Thor – they were all my best friends. But the ones I felt closest to were The X-Men. They were something totally unique. Not alien superheroes (like Superman) or changed by external forces (like Spider Man). They were real, born mutants. It was in their genes. For a natural outcast like myself the attraction is obvious. Make no mistake, the concept of The X-Men (it is, of course, an ongoing series with many variations) is one of the greatest masterpieces of this century.

2. *I am Legend* by Richard Matheson (novel). The best 'genre' works are adult fairytales. This horror/science fiction story comes from one of the Wizards of literature. Alienation has never been more

poetic, more barbaric. If you feel alone and misunderstood, this is your Bible. A must for all sexually confused geeks (like me).

3. *Myra Breckenridge* by Gore Vidal (novel). A nervous, male youth is sexually abused and raped by a transvestite wearing a dildo. The first novel that seriously turned me on. What more can I say?

4. *Dandelion Wine* by Ray Bradbury (novel). The greatest novel about childhood. Ever. Full-stop. No argument. It was one of the major inspirations behind my own film, *The Reflecting Skin*. Innocence is a dangerous magic.

5. *East of Eden* by John Steinbeck (novel). I sat up all night finishing it. I was fourteen. This book is as much part of me as the birthmark on my leg. The scope of it is breathtaking (that's the novel, not my birthmark). As a study of evil and (possible) redemption it's unparalleled. It's easy to knock this work as corny and sentimental. But, believe me, keep knocking and it'll let you in.

6. *The Collected Poems* by e e cummings (poetry). No writer has ever affected me like cummings. He changed the way I see the world. He changed me. There should be temples and cathedrals erected to him. Every child should recite 'Everyone lived in a pretty how town' instead of the Lord's Prayer. This poetry is about feeling beyond meaning. Ask not what it means, but what it makes you feel. Meaning is feeling. Amen.

7. *Preacher* by Garth Ennis and Steve Dillon (comic). This graphic novel is still in mid-flow as I write. One of the most perfect fusions of images and words in the history of comics. It's work such as this that defines our age. Like life itself, it's revolting, compulsive, hilarious and quite, quite Godless.

8. *The Godfather* by Mario Puzo (novel). When I was at school everyone was wanking to the sex scene at the wedding. My old paperback still falls open at page 26. Violence has never been so glamorous. My English teacher called it 'morally bankrupt'. What better recommendation do you want?

9. *Suddenly, Last Summer* by Tennessee Williams (stage play). Tennessee Williams is my favourite playwright. And this is my favourite play of his. Only *The Silence of the Lambs* comes close to rivalling its exploration of the destructive force of desire. We need the skin we see, we are either destroyed by that skin or *we* destroy *it*. Each man skins the thing he loves. Hallelujah!

10. *The Vivisector* by Patrick White (novel). Quite simply, the greatest novel in the English language. I've read it at least once a year since I was sixteen. To describe it would be as pointless as tap-dancing about a lithograph. Just experience this orgasm of reading. Everything else is merely sneezing.

11. *The Exorcist* by William Peter Blatty (novel). I read this when I was thirteen at a Warner Holiday Camp on the Isle of Sheppey. Few things in life have ever been more deliciously perfect. The novel changed the way I wrote for years. I gave it to my English teacher. He said, 'Don't you think it's a little . . . well, ripe?' Well, yes. That's the whole bloody point. Like a potent dream, the true effect is felt afterwards. In the aftertaste, not the eating. For that, ripeness is all. Besides, most so-called critics have no sense of alchemy. And this book (like the film) is alchemy through and through.

12. *The Collected Short Stories* by Robert Bloch (short stories). So much of what's happening in contemporary cinema started with Bloch. My whole teenaged life was spent reading and re-reading these stories. Masterpieces one and all. If you've never read 'Yours Truly, Jack the Ripper' . . . well, you just ain't lived!

13. *A Study in Scarlet* by Sir Arthur Conan Doyle (novel). The book that introduced the world to a queer, autistic drug addict: namely, Sherlock Holmes. I'd read every Sherlock Holmes story by the age of ten. Me and my best friend Mark called each other 'Holmes' and 'Watson' and would stroll up and down Bethnal Green Road hunting out crime. What found it's apotheosis in *The X-Files* started here. The scarlet of the title is blood, by the way.

14. *More Than Human* by Theodore Sturgeon (novel). No life is complete without experiencing this.

15. *The Paperboy* by Pete Dexter (novel). Ditto.

16. *Dust Tracks on the Road* by Zora Neale Hurston (novel). Ditto.

17. *The Annunciation* by Ellen Gilchrist (novel). Ditto.

18. *By Grand Central Station I Sat Down and Wept* by Elizabeth Smart (novel). Ditto.

19. *The Heart of Darkness* by Joseph Conrad (novella). Ditto.

20. *Alice's Adventures in Wonderland* by Lewis Carroll (novel). Ditto.

21. *A Canticle for Leibowitz* by Walter Miller (novel). Ditto.

22. *The Murder of Roger Ackroyd* by Agatha Christie (novel). Ditto.

23. *Flowers for Algernon* by Daniel Keyes (novel). Ditto.

24. *Happy Days* by Samuel Beckett (stage play). The older I get the more this means to me. As a teenager I found it ridiculous. In my twenties it was funny. Now it's heartbreaking. The closest any dramatic work has come to a ritual. In this case, the ritual of loss and decay. Oh, such happy days . . . such happy days . . .

25. *Daddy* by Sylvia Plath (poem). Whatever you think your favourite nihilistic band is doing, Plath got there first. She was losing her religion before REM's parents were twinkles in their parents' eyes. This was the first poem I learnt by heart. Like all Plath's work, it's a magical incantation and sparkles like polished bones.

26. *The Glamour* by Christopher Priest (novel). I love all of Priest's work. I single this out because its themes of love and loss are in my orbit at the moment. Priest's work is brave, inventive and . . . oh, just read him!

27. *Something Happened* by Joseph Heller (novel). Much better than

Catch-22 (which I've always found unreadable), this book has an ending that left me, quite literally, dizzy with shock and grief. Like Bellow and Amis (Jnr), Heller's prose is as addictive as any drug. Inject me.

28. *Goldfinger* by Ian Fleming (novel). I enjoy all the Bond books (in all their homophobic, snobbish, sexist, imperialistic, racist, anal glory) and this is the best. Of course, you have to play John Barry in the background. And wear a leather cat suit. Or is that just me?

29. *Interview with the Vampire* by Anne Rice (novel). The *One Hundred Years of Solitude* of horror fiction. Beautiful, seductive and as erotic as they come. (And I do mean cooommme!!)

30. *The Church of Dead Girls* by Stephen Dobyns (novel). This reads like *Peyton Place* meets *Seven*. Severed hands, masturbation, homosexuality and ear mastication. Pure delight. For me, this novel contains more beauty and religious power than the stained glass windows of Notre Dame Cathedral. It should be studied by every eight-year old as a lesson in the true nature of community.

31. *Cymbeline* by William Shakespeare (stage play). Sexier and more violent than a naked Brad Pitt stomping kittens while being wanked off by Uma Thurman.

32. *The Maids* by Jean Genet (stage play). My favourite artists have always been those whose work and life are inseparable. Genet is a prime example. Dark, dangerous, erotic. What are the new rituals we need to keep on living? Genet knows!

33. *Red Dragon* by Thomas Harris (novel). This came before *The Silence of the Lambs* and is every bit as chilling. I mention it here as an excuse to beat the drum about *Manhunter* (the film of the book, directed by Michael Mann), which contains the definitive portrayal of Hannibal Lecter by Brian Cox.

34. *The Three Stigmata of Palmer Eldritch* by Philip K. Dick (novel).

Dick is my favourite novelist and the one who's influenced me the most. If I start writing about him I won't know where to stop. Suffice to say, his work is mythical, haunting, brave and as inventive as Leonardo da Vinci after a bucket of sulphate. This is the real literature of this century. Miss it at your peril.

35. *The Penultimate Truth* by Philip K. Dick (novel). Ditto.

36. *UBIK* by Philip K. Dick (novel). Ditto.

37. *The Simulacra* by Philip K. Dick (novel). Ditto.

38. *Flow my Tears, the Policeman Said* by Philip K. Dick (novel). Ditto.

39. *The Man in the High Castle* by Philip K. Dick (novel). Ditto.

40. *Do Androids Dream of Electric Sheep* by Philip K. Dick (novel). Ditto.

41. *A Scanner Darkly* by Philip K. Dick (novel). Ditto.

42. *Valis* by Philip K. Dick (novel). Ditto.

43. *The Game-Players of Titan* by Philip K. Dick (novel). Ditto.

44. *Postmortem* by Patricia Cornwell (novel). Autopsies have never been more beautiful. A true original, with a prose style as smooth as hot scalpels through eyeballs.

45. *Vurt* by Jeff Noon (novel). Some writers you feel a particular infinity with. For me, Noon is one. I read him and think yeah, I've been there. I know that world. Needless to say, I think he's the bees knees. Or should I say, the dealer's feather?

46. *The Wizard of Oz* by Frank L. Baum (novel). Because it's there.

47. *Brokeback Mountain* by Annie Proulx (novella). Sex. Time. Loss. Self-deceit. Death. The story of my life, really. Few works have dared to be so brutally honest about male relationships. The terms 'gay', 'straight', 'bi-sexual' are totally redundant and have crippled our imaginations for too long. My nephew's bedroom is full of posters of Michael Owen and Michael Jackson. He knows. He understands.

Words must set us free. Invent new words for what we are. There should be hundreds of words for different shades of sexual and emotional need. This book can open the debate . . . if anyone's listening.

48. *Solomon Kane* by Robert E. Howard (short stories). Howard was years ahead of everyone. His *Solomon Kane* tales are the most exciting films never made. Dark, barbaric, sexy, this is imagist storytelling of the highest order.

49. *Peter Pan* by J. M. Barrie (novel). The greatest queer text ever. Fairies, lost boys, mermaids, a pirate, and a pretty boy who takes you back to his place, tells you he loves you, then forgets all about you – oh, perrr-leaze!!

50. *Rosemary's Baby* by Ira Levin (novel). Anything that mixes childhood with evil gets my vote. But an evil foetus! Who can resist? Anyone who's ever had a relationship with a 'nasty piece of work' knows what this novel is about. Sex can steal your very soul.

51. *Torso* by John Peyton Looke (novel). Murder. Queers. Chickens. Mutilations. I've been raving about this since I first read it. Out of the carnage emerges one of the most tender love stories ever! Swoon! Let me film it, somebody. I'd do a good job. Honest, guv.

52. *Arkham Asylum* by Morrison and McKean (graphic novel). This threw out the rule book and invented a new one. A darker one. A cruel one. I adore every twisted page.

53. *The Curse of the Starving Class* by Sam Shepard (stage play). Anything by Shepard is the most brutal magic. I've chosen this because it was the first I read! Nuff said.

54. *Station to Station* by David Bowie (album lyrics). Because he wrote them just for me!

55. *The Curse of Millhaven* by Nick Cave (song lyric). Because I wish I'd written it.

56. *The Sirens of Titan* by Kurt Vonnegut (novel). Life is meaningless. I always knew it.

57. *Earthly Powers* by Anthony Burgess (novel). More towering and majestic than five hundred Kings and Queens playing a game of 'Wear Stilts and Talk Majestically' on top of the Empire State Building.

58. *Frisk* by Dennis Cooper (novel). I can't believe that this is not a school text. It's everything good literature should be; beautifully written, expertly structured, and with complex characters. Of course, there's the sexual murder and mutilation of a young boy. Cooper is the Coleridge of butchery. And in schools – oh, they could learn so much.

59. *Childhood's End* by Arthur C. Clark (novel). Life isn't everything – I always knew it.

60. *In Cold Blood* by Truman Capote (novel). Something terrible happens to a family. You have to keep reading to find out what. The novel as cynical exploration . . . but written by an angel. Chilling and heavenly in equal measure. (Just like my last relationship, come to think of it.)

61. *Pet Sematary* by Stephen King (novel). When he's good, he's very, very good. And this is King at his best. It's the duty of horror to tackle our taboos. Here it's death. One of the most spine-tingling last lines ever. Heart-breaking and scary in equal measure. (Again, just like my last . . . etc. etc.)

62. *The Executioner's Song* by Norman Mailer (novel). More narrative drive than a juggernaut full of pulp fiction without breaks on a highway covered with ice.

63. *Wide Sargasso Sea* by Jean Rhys (novel). Quite simply, a prose style to die for. Seductive and intimidating in equal measure. (Just like my last – oh, what is wrong with me?!)

64. *Lost Souls* by Poppy Z. Brite (novel). When I was doing the

festival circuit with my film *The Reflecting Skin*, everyone kept telling me, 'You've got to film *Lost Souls*.' I hadn't read it at the time. But when I eventually did . . . oh, yes! It was like a love letter from my oldest friend!

65. Bill Hicks' Routines (stand-up comedy). Quite simply, I worship at his feet.

66. *The White Hotel* by D. M. Thomas (novel). When I was at college I went into the coffee bar one day and found a girl in hysterical tears. The reason? She'd just finished reading this book. It became a huge cult amongst my friends. Everyone read it. Everyone wept. I can't believe it's been so quickly forgotten. There was once a rumour it was going to be a David Lynch film starring Meryl Streep. One of the great cinematic experiences that never was.

67. *Saved* by Edward Bond (stage play). When I was at school we were told to write about a play of choice. I chose this. I got an E minus with the comment, 'Your subject matter let you down.' My journey as a writer started there.

68. *The Talented Mr Ripley* by Patricia Highsmith (novel). Makes moral ambiguity an art-form. A fable about the overwhelming force of consuming physical love – at least, that's what I think! Each man wants to become the thing he loves. Or kill it. Or be killed by it. Or have it become him.

69. *James and the Giant Peach* by Roald Dahl (novel). I didn't read many children's novels as a child. I was too busy with comics and horror. But once I started (in my late teens) I realised there was more sheer invention and pace in their pages than in most adult fiction. This novel is a case in point. It's here that institutions like the Booker Prize should be looking.

70. *Timothy of the Cay* by Theodore Taylor (novel). Ditto.

71. *The Indian in the Cupboard* by Lynne Reid Banks (novel). Ditto.

72. *His Dark Materials* trilogy by Philip Pullman (novels). Ditto.

73. *The Phantom Tollbooth* by Norman Juster (novel). Ditto.

74. *Stig of the Dump* by Clive King (novel). This is one book I did read as a child. As an invalid, yearning for friends, this had particular resonance for me. Where are you Stig? I'm still looking for you! How many dirty dumps do I have to search?

75. *Mary Poppins* by P. L. Travers (novel). This has always scared the shit out of me.

76. *And Death Shall Have No Dominion* by Dylan Thomas (poem). Discovering Thomas for the first time is like discovering sex: you can't believe you're feeling so much without knowing why. Like e e cummings, a Wizard of meaning over feeling. Oh, those unicorn evils!

77. *Gormenghast* trilogy by Mervyn Peake (novels and a half). Peake is one of the wildest Wizards of the twentieth century. Multi-talented and still misunderstood, he's a typical example of an artist who, because he can't be easily categorised, is all too easily ignored by the so-called critical establishment. What a crime. Honestly. A real crime. Make those responsible drink bleach!

78. *Our Mutual Friend* by Charles Dickens (novel). Everyone keeps telling me Dickens is plotless and sentimental. So what? He's got more talent in one whisker than all their cynical goatees.

79. *The Wasp Factory* by Iain Banks (novel). This is how I remember my own childhood: sick, funny, savage and sadistic. Besides, anything with cruelty to animals and a maggoty-brained baby *must* be a masterpiece.

80. *The Turn of the Screw* by Henry James (novella). Kids! Scared kids! Ghosts! Sex! Sexy ghosts! Ghostly kids! Scary kids! Sexy kids – oh, slap me! Slap me!

81. *The Midwich Cuckoos* by John Wyndham (novel). Evil kids! I can't resist! Society's fear of rebellious youth starts here.

82. *Spring Awakening* by Frank Wedekind (stage play). It's kids again!

83. *Wild Boys* by William S. Burroughs (novel). An experience like no other. If you're lucky, this book will really fuck you up.

84. *A Demon in my View* by Edgar Allan Poe (poem). If the twentieth century could write a poem, it'd be this one. I used it in the screenplay to the gangster film *The Krays*. 'From childhood's hour I have not been as others were . . .' You better believe it!

85. *Brimstone and Treacle* by Dennis Potter (teleplay). I remember watching this when it was first broadcast and thinking, Yes! I want to write like this! When my first stage play, *The Pitchfork Disney*, was premiered, I was petrified everyone would say, 'Oh it's just like *Brimstone and Treacle*.' But no one did. Goldfish memory or what? Critics compared it to everything (so long as it wasn't older than eighteen months) except the obvious. Here I put the record straight. Thanks, Dennis.

86. *All About Eve* by Joseph L. Mankiewicz (screenplay). Not the kind of screenplay I usually go for. It's wordy and not very cinematic. And yet . . . it sparkles like a jewel-encrusted razor blade. And, in film, Bette Davis is all the cinema you need.

87. *Vertigo* by Alec Coppel and Samuel Taylor (screenplay). The kind of screenplay I always go for. It tells the story from image to image. It's dreamlike and totally illogical. Alchemy of the purest kind.

88. *Taxi Driver* by Paul Schrader (screenplay). My favourite screenplay. When I first saw the film I nearly passed out at the bloodbath ending. Oh, the images! The music! The music with images! Ecstasy!

89. *The Vision of the Fool* by Cecil Collins (essays). Collins was my first art tutor and his influence on me was (and is) huge. He saw me struggling with a drawing one day. I asked him, 'What do you think?' He said, 'You'll always be lonely.' Perfection!

90. *In Search of our Mother's Gardens* by Alice Walker (Essays). More inspiring than flying a helicopter through the Grand Canyon while playing Beethoven's ninth Symphony and having Brad Pitt and Nicole Kidman sucking your toes and repeating, 'We are not worthy'!

91. *The Empty Space* by Peter Brook (essays). Ditto.

92. *Sexual Personae* by Camille Paglia (essays). Ditto.

93. *Star Trek* by Gene Rodenberry (TV series concept). Like a Renaissance painter sketching out a vast canvas (and letting others fill in the gaps), Rodenberry created one of the greatest 'concepts' of all time. This original canvas is sizeless and can encompass almost anything. Long may it expand.

94. *The Iliad* by Homer (storytelling). Obviously.

95. *The Odyssey* by Homer (storytelling). Again, obviously.

96. *A Matter of Life and Death* by Oscar Moore (????). The first interview I ever gave was with Oscar. We got on like a house on fire. I never had a chance to tell him how much I loved this book before he died. So I do so now. You did it before me, you clever bastard.

97. *The Little Prince* by Antoine de Saint-Exupéry (novel and then some). This book is like the start of a new religion.

98. *Elvissey* by Jack Womack (novel). I ended a relationship with someone because they didn't like this book. Some things are that important.

99. *Tales of Mystery and Imagination* by Edgar Allan Poe (short stories). Twentieth-century writing starts here.

100. *A Life in Movies* by Michael Powell (autobiography). Powell helped shape my idea of what film can do. Like all true visionaries, he was often savaged by critics, ignored by the public and generally ridiculed. But without brave explorers like him there is no artistic future. It's the artist who risks a shipwreck who discovers new

islands. It's only in the dark we stumble over anything new. Turn the lights off! Step forward! Explore . . .

PHILIP RIDLEY *is the author of novels for both children and adults, as well as a number of screenplays and plays.*

Jon Riley

What is your definition of a classic?

My definition of a 'classic' novel is a book that has stood the test of time, remained in print, is esteemed by other writers and has provoked a degree of critical interest. The test of time is a hopelessly arbitrary standard; my barrier is twenty-five years. It could with equal reason be a bit more or less. Examples of writers who have attained this status are Patrick Hamilton and Henry Green. Their work has been frequently reissued and finds a small but renewed readership, other writers insist upon their achievement and they have positions in the history of twentieth-century English literature, albeit as minor figures. Alternatively, their contemporary Joyce Cary has failed to make the cut despite enthusiasts and occasional reissues.

I am not sure that the term is very useful anymore. The notion that the passage of time is relevant to the accuracy of the claim that something is a classic is ignored and the word has been appropriated into the vocabulary of marketing.

Yet in spite of this I can't think of a term that suggests literary status – quality, influence and longevity – any better, so the term should remain, even if it is used to describe *Pocahontas* on video and compilations of heavy-metal hits.

For me an early aversion to classics was inflamed by premature exposure to Sir Walter Scott's *Ivanhoe*, which I read without pleasure or comprehension. From then on 'classic' meant BBC television serials on long Sunday afternoons, the works of Mrs Gaskell, Scott (again!), Stevenson and others brought to a small black and white screen. Dickens was an exception due to frightening old films like *Oliver Twist* and *David Copperfield* and *A Christmas Carol.* He made me realise that classic books need not be viciously dull and was the first classic writer I truly loved.

I am not sure who is deliberately writing with an eye on the twenty-first century, although the deliberateness of his style and the thorough vividness of his worlds and the realisation of the humanity of his characters mean that Graham Swift's work is, I think, very likely to endure; I feel similarly about Kazuo Ishiguro's fiction. For different reasons I believe that Don DeLillo's work will be important, largely because his language seems to reflect very exactly states of mind in the late twentieth century.

Equally, I am unsure what will assure readership in the next century, but there will have to be a quality in language which makes one book come alive to future generations and the lack of which makes another expire. Just as subjective is the way the novel affects you. A writer once said to me that the test of a really good book is that it can change, by the tiniest degree, the way the reader subsequently looks at the world. Most of the writers whose work I hope will gain them classic status have this alchemical ability to fuse language with imagination, regardless of immediate political or historical implications. That is why Evelyn Waugh is still one of the great novelists of the century, even though his political and religious views seem quite alien to most of his readers today.

What are your ten essential classic novels for the next 100 years?

Which writers will last in the next hundred years – this is the difficult bit. I think I will try to limit myself to writers of the last twenty-five years, as there seems to be reasonable consensus about the status of the writers of the first three quarters of the century and I feel like being a pundit.

Waterland by Graham Swift. This is a novel which feels so steeped in history, tradition and folklore that it seems almost indecent to have in addition an emotional range and narrator that fully involve the reader.

Money by Martin Amis. Its swagger and fusion of language – slang, neologisms, Amis-speak – have meant that *Money* is one of the most influential novels of the last twenty years. It also was hugely ambitious in attempting to nail down the consumption mania of the Bolly-and-BMW era.

The Birthday Boys by Beryl Bainbridge. A great story of foolish courage given human scale, characters whose voices speak as if across myth and decades. The strength of emotion in the final pages is so breathtaking that coming away from the novel was like being released from a spell.

Trainspotting by Irvine Welsh. The most influential novel of the last decade and in it Welsh did what very few writers can do – he created the taste by which he is judged.

What a Carve-Up! by Jonathan Coe. Long after the political relevance is past this has an architectural beauty of construction and a plot that Wilkie Collins would have tipped his hat to.

The Blue Flower by Penelope Fitzgerald. Nothing I have read in fiction makes the sensibility of romanticism so clear to me, even more so as it is so rooted in late-eighteenth-century Germany that it makes one believe that the book could have been written two hundred years ago.

White Noise by Don DeLillo. No one, not even Roth or Updike, writes of the phobias and preoccupations of the greatest power in history with such precision and electric style. This novel will show the reader of the twenty-first century that the author of *Underworld* also had a great comic side.

The Remains of the Day by Kazuo Ishiguro. This is as near faultless as I can imagine a novel to be. Its elegance, sadness, sensitivity and humanity are always there, never on show, part of the writer's mysterious art.

Life: A User's Manual by George Perec. Even in translation, its linguistic brilliance and game-playing come through; underneath the glittering surface is deep feeling for what used to be known as the human condition.

A Suitable Boy by Vikram Seth. This will be read in a hundred years' time for reasons that are similar to Dickens's enduring appeal – its vast canvas, its humanity and its fantastic fidelity to human nature.

What are the books you believe should never have been called classics?

These books listed below have not, I think, deserved the status they have; I ought to add that several of the authors listed nearly made it into my top ten with different novels:

The Bonfire of the Vanities by Tom Wolfe

Vineland by Thomas Pynchon

Foucault's Pendulum by Umberto Eco

Last Exit to Brooklyn by Hubert Selby Jnr.

Portnoy's Complaint by Philip Roth

The Moor's Last Sigh by Salman Rushdie

G by John Berger

How Late it was, How Late by James Kelman

The Mezzanine by Nicholson Baker

It is very hard to generalise about this group, suffice to say that they are highly praised books by writers not at their best – how dogmatic can I get?

JON RILEY *is Chief Editor at the publishers Faber and Faber.*

Harry Ritchie

What is your definition of a classic?

It used to be easy to define a classic – if it was written by somebody who was long since dead, and if you had to study it at school or university and/or it bored the pants off you, then a book was definitely a classic. And even though it might be shite (eg Cyril Connolly's *The Rock Pool*), a book was unarguably a 'modern classic' if it was published by Penguin in a grey cover and with, lest there have lingered any doubt about the matter, the logo 'Penguin Modern Classic'.

Now, however, the whole business of sorting literature out into categories of worth is confused and messy – and quite right too. Although many people instinctively want and need to have a defined canon of greatness, with writers graded in the literary equivalent of a squash ladder (Shakespeare at the top, Milton the runner-up, Wordsworth at three, Chaucer four, George Eliot five, right down to the lowest rung occupied by Barbara Cartland), the uncomfortable truth is that literary judgment can't be definitive and objective. It makes absolutely no sense whatsoever to say, 'Shakespeare is the greatest writer in the language.' What you can say is this: 'In my opinion, Shakespeare is the greatest writer in the language.' That's why those 'Who's better – Keats or Bob Dylan?' debates are so daft. Any such question is unanswerable. (Actually, come to think of it, that particular question isn't worth discussing because Bob Dylan is the exception that proves the rule, being, by any sane criterion, mince.)

What are your ten essential classic novels for the next 100 years?

Having said all that, here's a list of ten novels, published in the Nineties, that will be classics – i.e. that I think are terrific and that I hope will still be read, and with a sense of what life and literature are like now, in a hundred or two hundred years' time:

Trainspotting by Irvine Welsh

Enduring Love by Ian McEwan

Bridget Jones's Diary by Helen Fielding

The Robber Bride by Margaret Atwood

Larry's Party by Carol Shields

Morvern Callar by Alan Warner

About a Boy by Nick Hornby

Felicia's Journey by William Trevor

Last Orders by Graham Swift

The Van by Roddy Doyle

Significantly, what these books have in common, apart from the fact that I reckon they're brilliant, is that so many other people clearly think they're brilliant as well, because they have all sold lots of copies – some of them lots and lots of copies. This is the proof that the old assumption – that only garbage sells – is simply wrong. Look at any best-seller list of recent years and you'll find that at least half the books in it will not be derided schlock but the kind of books that get great reviews and win lots of prizes. Only a disgusting sycophant would use this particular opportunity to wax lyrical about one of the reasons for this being the superb developments, in the Eighties and Nineties, of the book-retail trade, so I won't mention it.

What are the books you believe should never have been called classics?

Compare and contrast that list of terrific and popular novelists with the following list of books that are supposed to be classics, but only by people running English Lit. courses. What people running English Lit. courses prize above all else are things which they can claim to discover – deep-lying patterns of image and symbol, cunningly concealed significance – as if the highest function of literature is to offer clues to spot and puzzles to solve. What people running English Lit. courses don't like, or mistrust or dismiss as of no importance, are qualities like plot, story, humour, characterisation, insight and sheer readability. Which explains why the following 'classics' are notable for their phenomenal commitment to tedium: *Pamela* by Samuel Richardson, *Wuthering Heights* by Emily Brontë, *Daniel Deronda* by George Eliot, The Collected Works (even the dirty bits) of D. H. Lawrence, The Collected Fiction of Virginia Woolf, *Ulysses* by James Joyce, *Finnegans* (fucking) *Wake* by James Joyce, *The Egoist* by George Meredith, *Nostromo* by Joseph Conrad, and, last and least, *The Golden Bowl* by Henry James.

HARRY RITCHIE *is the former Literary Editor of the* Sunday Times *and the author of* The Last Pink Bits.

Boyd Tonkin

What is your definition of a classic?

No one put the case against them better than Henry Miller. 'Every man with a bellyful of classics,' wrote the *enfant terrible* turned dirty old man of US fiction, 'is an enemy of the human race.'

You, and I, know exactly whom he means: the pedagogues, the syllabus-setters, the literary trainspotters, the you-won't-like-this-but-it-does-you-good brigade. 'Classic' in this killjoy sense means the urge to raise the dead in order to smother the living – worse, not to resurrect the thrilling mess of the real past, but to tidy it up into a tombstone row of examiners and librarians. Let's pause there. Henry Miller passed a long writing life in a state of constant mutiny against this kind of fixed order: sixty years kicking (as it were) against the pricks. Yet could even he, by some horrible mischance, have joined the phantom horde of 'classic' worthies? And, if so, how?

As I write, the hottest movie on release in Britain is Terry Gilliam's high-octane, goggle-eyed interpretation of *Fear and Loathing in Las Vegas*. Now, Hunter S. Thompson's uproarious trip (in every sense) from 1973 hardly burst onto the scene out of a clear blue Nevada sky. Consider the libidinous excess of its prose . . . the wayward stream-of-consciousness . . . the reckless blend of memoir and fantasy . . . the anarchic revolt against bourgeois manners and morals . . . Insofar as Thompson's wild child has a literary granddaddy, it could well be Miller's own *Tropic of Cancer* (the source, in fact, of our opening quotation).

Indeed, the ever-scandalous Henry took his first steps into the classic role of mentor and model fairly early on. George Orwell met him in Paris in the 1930's and came to admire his work (which was banned in Britain at the time). Toned down a bit for prim prewar Britain, Miller's freewheeling, convention-crashing voice allowed Orwell to write his novel *Coming Up for Air* in 1938. Then, in Miller's cantankerous old age, he found a kindred spirit of a different sort: Erica Jong, who later wrote a book about their friendship. She did to him what passionate readers and writers always do to real (as opposed to set-text) classics: not to approve or challenge them, but to use them gleefully and shamelessly, even against the grain of their intentions. Without Miller's *Tropic* books, no *Fear of Flying*.

Hunter S. Thompson, George Orwell, Erica Jong: flung together at a party, the trio could scarcely have exchanged a civil word. But books connect them, across decades, across cultures – even across gender. So the classics-hater grew into one himself: a fairly minor example of the type, maybe, but still with that crucial capacity to light a fire of fresh ideas in distant minds. The Italian fabulist Italo Calvino, who will surely survive into the next century as a classic of this one, defined a classic as 'a book that has never finished saying what it has to say'. 'Never' overstates the case a bit, perhaps: but it certainly goes on speaking to readers (and writers) for whom it was not at first intended. It gloriously overshoots its target audience. It talks to you, although it was not meant for you. Literature, as the poet Ezra Pound put it in a classic soundbite, is news that stays news. If this unplanned power to reach out and touch remote readers helps to pinpoint a classic achievement, it follows that the mere desire to write in a 'classic' tradition can never do the job by itself. In this respect, I think that the fractured world of modern fiction may differ from other genres – especially poetry. Harold Bloom, who has thought longer and harder about classics and canons than any other critic of our age, views the major poets wrestling with their ancestors in a conscious bid to match or rival them. This 'anxiety of influence' locks the greats in a chain of creative combat from Virgil to Eliot – or from Ovid to Ted Hughes, to cite an impressive recent confirmation of Bloom's line.

I believe that, in a diverse, democratic culture, fiction can only opt for a more accidental kind of immortality. When Evelyn Waugh came to compose *Brideshead Revisited*, he already had one eye trained on the 'Modern Classics' shelf (and another on a handsome book-club deal in the States). Too overt a worry about tradition (on the one hand) and posterity (on the other) bred a very classy – but not classic – form of backward-looking kitsch. The truly classic Waugh emerges from the screwed-up young drifter of *Decline and Fall* and *Vile Bodies*. Any frantic clubber or bewildered graduate can meet themselves in those books. To make the overripe nostalgia of *Brideshead* speak to us again took a luscious TV serial with the assembled forces of Jeremy Irons, John Gielgud, Laurence Olivier, a theme-tune you caught like a virus and the most irritating teddy-bear in artistic history. Any old book (or dead book) can become an ersatz 'classic' thanks to the costly exhumation practised by the big and small screeens. The real thing may need learned editors and cheap editions, but it retains the right to stalk our imaginations without those artificial aids. Jane Austen, a disregarded nobody in her time, can do just that – and did before the tidal wave of recent adaptations. Yet Walter Scott, a European superstar of precisely the same time, now lives on merely in stage or screen versions of his work – from Joan Sutherland's *Lucia di Lammermoor* to Liam Neeson's *Rob Roy*.

What are your ten essential classic novels for the next 100 years?

Around 1817 (the date of *Rob Roy*'s publication, and *Persuasion*'s completion), every educated person across the continent 'knew' that the Laird of Abbotsford had written classics. Possibly four people on the planet suspected that the Hampshire parson's daughter had. Predictions of future classic status have a track-record that's worse than risible. Risking the certain raspberries of posterity, I have chosen ten potential classics for well into the next century from novels by British or Northern Irish authors published in the last twenty years of this one: nothing, in other words, published earlier than 1980. The foremost peril of classics-tipping is that scale and hype seduce. You pick the *Rob Roy*s over the *Persuasion*s. I have probably fallen straight into that trap; although I wonder if any current critic could boast an Austen-spotting feature on his or her radar. But somewhere, I'm quite sure, will be an avid reader who can.

Future classics from the past 20 years:

Earthly Powers by Anthony Burgess (1980). Modernist epic meets airport-stall blockbuster in a comic, panoramic sweep of twentieth-century culture and history.

Lanark: a Life in Four Books by Alasdair Gray (1981). Abrasively funny in content, adventurous in form, Gray gives creative shape to the stricken industrial metropolis.

Midnight's Children by Salman Rushdie (1981). A landmark for post-imperial writers, and a master-class in making fiction match the modern world's plurality.

Empire of the Sun by J. G. Ballard (1984). The weird imaginings of a huge SF talent finally come to rest in a picture of his own traumatic wartime childhood.

Money by Martin Amis (1984). The comic epitome of late-century market forces, forged from a scabrous wit that launched a fleet of wannabes.

Oranges are not the Only Fruit by Jeanette Winterson (1985). The great English growing-up novel revisited to embrace sexual diversity, in a knowing and slyly erudite voice.

Dunedin by Shena Mackay (1990). The era's boldest comic artist deepens her tone, widens her scope, and explores the past forces that still shape us.

Downriver by Iain Sinclair (1991). A cult phantasmagoria of urban satire, occult lore and social fury, mixed into a fin-de-siecle *Tristram Shandy*.

The Regeneration Trilogy by Pat Barker (1991-95). The lasting traumas of the early century illuminated in lightning-flashes, with compassion and control, at its end.

Reading in the Dark by Seamus Deane (1996). Entrancing proof of the fertile new liaison between fiction and memoir, in the delicate record of an Irish boyhood.

What are the books you believe should never have been called classics?

Any fool can wreck *Macbeth* or *Middlemarch* by poor interpretation and wretched explanation. They remain true classics, even if some nasty encounter has ruined them for you. But which fêted texts should never have joined the immortals in the first place? Here are half a dozen twentieth-century idols to cross off your reading list:

Lady Chatterley's Lover by D. H. Lawrence. Actually, the sex provides about the only halfway-decent passages. The rest (like most late Lawrence) balloons into a sort of huge goitre made up of hysterical hot air.

Finnegans Wake by James Joyce. A kind of literary miracle: the ultimate failure in modern literature, from the writer who (in three separate genres) had formerly achieved the ultimate success.

Lucky Jim by Kingsley Amis. Patron saint of club bigots-turned *Loaded* lads sets the tone for forty years of boorish philistinism. Also from 1954, Iris Murdoch's *Under the Net* is much, much wittier.

Lord of the Flies by William Golding. A gift to sadistic schoolmasters who wanted to dress up their own cruel fantasies as evergreen 'truths' about human nature. Not timeless wisdom, but postwar panic.

The Catcher in the Rye by J. D. Salinger. The perfect read for adolescents of any age more enthralled by themselves than books: a narcissistic echo-chamber for generations of rich, navel-gazing teens.

The Colour Purple by Alice Walker. The *Uncle Tom's Cabin* of its age (and the most-taught book on US campuses). Citing Walker and Toni Morrison together is like bracketing Lulu with Jessye Norman.

BOYD TONKIN *is the Literary Editor of the* Independent.

Janey Walker

What is your definition of a classic?

I can't define a classic novel – beyond a classic being a book that has qualities which make it last beyond its time.

I don't think many writers are thinking ahead to the twenty-first century when they write. Nor should they. But great books will still have an audience if they say something about a place or a time or how we relate to one another. If I think of the 'classics', I have in my mind the books that have taken me into another world and another way of thinking. Those qualities will still hold good in the future.

What are your ten essential classic novels for the next 100 years?

The Life and Times of Michael K by J. M. Coetzee. The story of a man taking his mother back to the countryside in South Africa, a haunting and harsh glimpse of a country at war. But at the same time, it's very humane and gentle and beautiful, worth many re-readings.

Blood Meridian by Cormac McCarthy. One of the most violent books I've ever read – but it gives an extraordinary vision of how the West was really won. The book is set along the Texas-Mexican border in the 1850's, a murderous world of real outlaws and Indians that bears no relation to the mythology of the Wild West. His style of writing takes you into such a different world, right down to another level of existence and survival.

Earthly Powers by Anthony Burgess. An epic book spanning sixty years, stunning in its language and ambition and knowledge. I read it at school, too young to take it in, and am very glad I was reacquainted with it later.

O Pioneers! by Willa Cather. A book that's a delight to read and tells you more about the American Dream than any urban novel could. It's the story of immigrants on the Nebraska prairies fighting to make their land prosper, with wonderful descriptions of the land and the loneliness and the bitter struggle to keep going.

A Far Cry from Kensington by Muriel Spark. The world of England in the Fifties so acutely observed, with characters you think your parents must have known. Gentle and sharp by turn, with wit delivered in such an effortless fashion it seems almost accidental.

Vanity Fair by Thackeray. Still as modern and sharp as ever, proving that well-observed relationships and hypocrisies outlast their era and are as relevant a hundred years later.

And Quiet Flows the Don by Mikhail Sholokhov. The book that introduced me to the beauty and atmosphere of the great Russian epics.

Bleak House by Charles Dickens. If I can only choose one Dickens, it would be *Bleak House*: the characters, the places, the atmosphere, the way the book transports you to Victorian England and still seems so modern.

U.S.A. by John Dos Passos. A huge sprawling book chronicling the first quarter of the twentieth century in America, weaving clips of newsreel alongside real and fictional characters to give a real sense of the excitement and uncertainty.

Midnight's Children by Salman Rushdie

What are the books you believe should never have been called classics?

You ask for books that have been described as classics and shouldn't have been. Sorry – I don't feel strongly there are particular books that have been misrepresented.

JANEY WALKER *is Commissioning Editor for Arts at Channel 4 Television.*

Alan Warner

What is your definition of a classic?

I'm suspicious about the concept of classic novels *for* the twenty-first century because I don't think novels can be about new areas, dystopian concepts, technology, fashion, pseudo-scientific speculation, or intellectual themes at all. For me, novels must always start with character and be about journeys and turmoil within consciousness, or, if you like, the heart: novels are about emotions, politics and passions for freedom in people who could be us; people in peril upon all manner of depths, people acting the way we all might in those circumstances. Novels are part of this big, sometimes wonderful, sometimes woeful trip we're on. A great book weaves its seductive tale and by dint of the novel form's hopeless generosity, 'their' story becomes our story. I don't think it is you and I, the readership, who will have to respond more fully and with more passion, to the books around us, in what will become an increasingly philistine, increasingly materialistic, MTV-attention-span, sound-bite ruled twenty-first-century Europe. All artists can try to do is create as authentically as they possibly can at this moment. You write out of your times. You might be for or against them but you still write out of them. 'I despise my times,' Antoine de Saint Exupéry wrote, and right enough, his times killed him. His bracelet was recently found washed up on a beach near Marseilles; they've resumed the search for his sunken fighter aircraft, where his skull must have tapped gently in the rotted cockpit for half this century.

I suppose we should distinguish between the term 'classical' and 'classic'. To me the classical novel refers to the seventeenth- and eighteenth-century French novel concerned with order, proportion and resolution, *The Princess of Cleves* (1678) by Marie de Lafayette being the most perfectly beautiful.

I guess the term classic as applied to the novel today derives from the study of Greek and Latin texts and the 'classical' cultures of ancient Greece and Rome. It's been an astounding intellectual upheaval that for centuries in Europe the study of 'The Classics' in Greek and Latin was the normal approach to an education in the humanities. Since perhaps the First World War, few learn ancient Greek or Latin. Think of poor young Jude Fawley, nose buried in the dialects until Arabella whacked him on the cheek with a severed pig's penis! Today we don't read the Latin and Greek classics, even in translation. When I was sixteen, I let Nietzsche's criticism of the Greeks save me from bothering to read them! I once read *The Satyricon* by Petronius, but only because I saw the Fellini movie first. I read *The Golden Ass*, but only because I'd been told it was scatologically hilarious. I've read *Ulysses* about four or five times but *The Odyssey* only once and probably never will again. Aye, what does this say about us Moderns? We're a terrible bunch and we've a lot to answer for but some of us still read novels, especially the novels we allowed to inherit the value judgment: classic, like the ancient Greek and Roman tests, denoting something that has inherent and great value; something that will endure for all human beings regardless of race, nationality, gender and class, across vast periods of time, still retaining this essence of value. Important and excellent, classic novels are supposed to become standards for other artists to aspire to but never quite equal. Mmmm.

I'm pretty skeptical about this term classic when it has been appropriated in our century and applied to the very modern art form of novels in a very Euro-centric and often nationalistic manner. I think the 'granting' of classic status to a novel often has far less to do with some genuine formal significance or inherent value in that novel and more to do with the cultural, social and political context of how the novel has been 'read' in our century and the social class interests of those who deem the novel a classic.

At least the passing of time gives a perspective with which to view a writer's complete work; so now in 'British' literature we find whole swathes of nineteenth-century English novels are claimed as classic. *All* Austen, *all* Walter Scott, *all* Gaskell, *all* George Eliot, *all* of Dickens, *all* of Trollope – I don't have any argument against the reading of these novelists, but I think some of the great nineteenth-century British writers only produced a few first-rate novels (and some, like Scott, none!), yet publishers are quick to have *all* Dickens's work, even including inferior stuff like *Pictures of Italy*, advertised under the classic imprint. Just because certain writers produced a few, profoundly influential novels, it doesn't make their entire body of work 'classic', constantly choking the shelves of most high street stores. This gives a lot of minor work by nineteenth-century English novelists (the poetry of the Brontës!) and innumerable medieval tests a classic status which often seems just to be on the strength of their antiquity. A sort of snob-status-cum-heritage-industry is going on here that seems questionable when some of that work is held up against many less well-known writers from other parts of the world. For instance, I would argue that Benito Perez Galdos (1843–1920), the Spanish novelist, has written many finer novels than Charles Dickens, but we never see that expressed on British bookshelves. I've lived in Dublin for some time now and it's interesting to see a Penguin Classic layout in a large bookshop here. Less self-conscious about the status of English nineteenth-century classics, the stocked books are refreshingly more varied and international.

So classics take on a nationalistic bias, the way a country tries to boast about its GNP or its scenery. You could defend this state of affairs by saying it's to do with the English language, which is bound to give a bias towards England's own novels. If it's about language, then I would challenge you to find a copy of the American writer Theodor Dreiser's remarkable *An American Tragedy* (1925). I searched for ten years to get a copy and finally found one two days into my first visit to New York.

Things become even more questionable when awarding the twentieth-century novel as a classic. Who is telling us this or that novel is a 'twentieth-century' or 'modern' classic or the giveaway 'Oxford World Classic'? At random I'm picking up an Oxford World Classic and looking at the 'Other Oxford *World* Classics' advertised in the back pages. Their select list is: Austen, J. M. Barrie, Beckford, Bunyan, Carlyle, Chaucer, Dickens, Edgeworth, Gaskell, Hardy, Homer, Ibsen, Henry James, Jocelin of Brakelond, Ben Jonson, Leonardo da Vinci, Melville, Prosper Merimée, Edgar Allan Poe, Mary Shelley, Bram Stoker, Trollope, Wilde and Woolf. Notice the unbiased, democratic alphabetical order, but if we designate Carlyle and Barrie as Scottish, and Stoker, Wilde and Edgeworth as Irish writers (who are frequently hi-jacked as examples of the English novel where 'English' subtly comes to mean the country rather than the language!), out of twenty-four writers, twelve are English! It makes the '*World*' monicker ring a little hollow. It's almost as if this canon of worthy reading is trying to *keep* us away from other great writers from around the world. Internationalism isn't doing too well at Oxford 'World' Classics.

So who decides it's a classic? The readership? Our schools? Who told them? Is it the moribund, conservative academia of the universities who invariably introduce each novel (and, have you noticed, always bloody tell you what the ending is)? I think critics, like the bewilderingly influential F. R. Leavis (who tried, xenophobically, to claim Richardson's *Clarissa* was a greater novel than all Proust!) or Harold Bloom, have done immense damage with their ridiculous, prescriptive 'canons' of great writing, promulgating the quasi-mystical position that these works contain some inherent 'value' or 'essence' that will transfer, like a flu virus, on to all readers.

I believe classic novels can exist without establishing a canon of deified novels that people are forced to read and think of as 'improving' and in some way valuable without reference to the reader's history or lived, contemporary reality. The danger of setting up canons and deciding works are morally improving is obvious. Are we really daring to infer that someone who has *not* read any particular canon we might choose (Shakespeare, Samuel Richardson, all of Proust, Brazilian novels or Japanese novels or the poems of Burns), are we really daring to suggest this person is lacking something . . . is in fact inferior? If I think *Jude the Obscure* is melodramatic, poorly written, lumberingly badly paced and out-dated, where does the fault lie? Do I have to do the explaining or does Hardy? We are made to feel something is inadequate with *us* if we dispute the value of a classic, yet perhaps the problem resides in the work, not the reader who brings so much of his or her own experience to it.

We remain surrounded by novels claiming to be classics. Is it just publishers trying to shift units of material now in the Public Domain? Are we really going to leave Penguin Classics and Oxford Classics to have the final word, because they print the word 'classic' on the paperback cover? Are we going to allow them the monopoly? Certainly not, because novels can take on classic status within certain countries and even among communities and groups. Classic status can be accorded whenever like-minded readers communicate.

I'm thinking of the way Nobel-winner Haldor Laxness's great novels, *The Atom Station* (1948) and *Independent People* (1946), are revered in Iceland but virtually unknown elsewhere. I'm thinking of the great Scottish poet, Iain Crichton Smith. His historical novel, *Consider the Lilies* (1969), dealing with the ethnic cleansing that occurred in the Scottish Highlands in the eighteenth and nine-teenth century (it was on the syllabus at my high school), is certainly considered a classic amongst many people in the Highlands and their Diaspora in Canada. Geographically its classic status doesn't even carry down to the Scottish cities. Think of the reputation of Wladyslaw Reymont's *The Peasants* (1902–1909) in Poland, or George Duhamel's in France. They are indisputably major (a word I prefer to 'classic') writers but their reputations and translations are in woeful shape in Britain.

I believe not only can a community decide a novel is classic, an individual can as well. I think for a novel to be considered classic, we must just personally be deeply moved by it, in a big way. We shouldn't just be told we must like it because 'it's a classic'; we must feel it. This means we can't accept a novel is classic just on intellectual and cultural grounds. If it doesn't affect us, if it doesn't get under our skin and into our emotions, we have the right to dismiss it. We should consider what F. Scott Fitzgerald wrote about novelists and himself:

> We have two or three great moving experiences in our lives – experiences so great and moving that it doesn't seem at the time that anyone else has been caught up and pounded and dazzled and astonished and beaten and broken and rescued and illuminated and rewarded and humbled in just that way.
>
> Then we learn our trade, well or less well, and we tell our two or three stories – each time in a new disguise – maybe ten times, maybe a hundred, as long as people will listen . . . Whether it's something that happened twenty years ago or only yesterday, I must start out with an emotion – one that's close to me and that I can understand.

It's the communication of this emotion that I'm advocating as the touchstone of a classic novel. It's personal; it's to do with your existence and the way you live life, what you think literature should do and how a text affects you. If you think it's formally just an old melodrama or if it's just boring, that's up to you. It makes the definition terribly subjective but when isn't the allocation of a novel as a classic ultimately subjective? It's up to each one of us if a work is a classic or not.

This is why excellent publishing ventures like Rebel Inc's 'Underground Classics' and Serpent's Tail's 'Extraordinary Classics' series, and genuine, unbiased international lists like that of the London publishers Harvill, are so important. Series of novels like this show the swirls and eddies of alternative views as to what is an international classic novel and challenge how, socially and culturally, novels become classics. Classics for whom? What does *Brideshead Revisited* mean to an unemployed single mother living in a damp run-down orbital housing estate south of Glasgow? What does *Trainspotting* mean to a privately educated Hampshire man earning £180,000 per year? What does *The Way We Live Now* by Trollope mean to a street kid in Brazil? The idea that *all* classic novels contain some mysterious essence of 'value' and 'improvement' that will universally leap out of the paper and begin edifying the passive opener of the pages, becomes highly questionable in a world torn with outrageous social inequalities. Classics are an open book.

What are your ten essential classic novels for the next 100 years?

The Devil to Pay in the Backlands (1954) by Joao Guimareas Rosa. I forced myself to choose between this and Joyce's *Ulysses* and finally went for this, because really I think it's greater and I love a dip into *Ulysses* very, very much! Probably the most neglected novel of the twentieth century, I can only hope the twenty-first will give it the recognition it's been denied in this one, especially in Thomas Colchie's forthcoming new translation. Set in the Brazilian wilds, it's really a savage hunt for revenge after the narrator has made a pact with the devil. Guimareas Rosa invented a new language for the backlanders, conveying their complexity. The novel is one of the greatest Latin-American novels, yet it's ridiculously obscured by lesser works; its vigour and its depth along with its sweeping surreality will effortlessly carry it into the next century.

The Shipyard (1961) by Juan Onetti. A far more important writer than Carpentier, Isabel Allende, Fuentes or Garcia Marquez, Onetti's deeply misanthropic vision and brilliantly elusive but realist style didn't fit in with the more exotic requirements of the 1970s 'magical realism' boom of English-translated Latin American novels. Onetti became a secret best kept (as did Miguel Asturias) by the accordance of overnight classic status to others. Across a sequence of ever more original novels, Onetti created Santa Maria, a tangible geographical universe, and he had a unified, heart-rending view of human behaviour that's never without a raunchy, black, gallows humour. A powerful attack on capitalism and First-World neglect and a wicked parody of Austen and the 'society' novel, *The Shipyard* has at its centre the ever sardonic Larsen, gold-digging to marry the shipyard owner, old Petrus's insane daughter; as you do in a land where poverty means the pauper's grave. Will he succeed or not? Everything is so ultimately hopeless it's not without humour. The rusting shipyard has gone bust but everyone acts as if it's a prestigious place to work with an illustrious future; Larsen's completely destitute and backbiting co-workers haven't received pay, maybe for years, but carry on in the hope that one day they'll see some actual cash. All is phantasms or chimeras or Larsen's thwarted, sour dreams; reality is cigarettes to stave off hunger until the next pot of communal stew, with failure, winter and death waiting always just hours away.

Molloy, Malone Dies and *The Unnameable* (1951–1953) by Samuel Beckett. The funniest stuff ever written. Simultaneously deprecatingly down-to-earth, deeply hilarious (the *Times Literary Supplement* has never been put to better use than wrapped and layered tightly around Molloy's lower torso, to conceal the pungent forcefulness of his farts) yet still mysterious and profound, the trilogy leads us into one of the great breakthroughs of twentieth-century literature – the destruction and eventual elimination of Narrative. Though anticipated by Onetti's *El Pozo* (1939), the trilogy destroys what the novel had always been about, 'telling stories', yet it turns this seemingly nihilistic move round, into a supreme act of creative generosity, launching the Novel off on other, seemingly infinite trajectories. Beckett's influence on the novel will last right into the twenty-first century and beyond. As a writer it's impossible to ignore him, yet most postwar English novelists have been unable to accept Beckett or Joyce. I chewed over this more famous one or that other great Irish trilogy, Eugene McCabe's shorter *Fermanagh* trilogy (1976–78).

The True Story of Ah-Q (1926) by Lu Sun. I made myself choose between this and *The Great Wall of China* by Franz Kafka, but since we're keeping the twenty-first century in mind, let's have this and think what role China itself is going to play in the twenty-first century. It's the similarity to Kafka I always see in this surprising, hysterical novel, with the lovable and completely mad rogue, Ah-Q, as its main character. For me this short novel encapsulates an unfathomably vast country, like the Kafka story, but makes its population tangible, almost familiar. We should look more closely at Chinese writing when we try to imagine what China's going to mean to the world in the next century. Nowhere are the lies of limitless economic expansionism as a virtue more absurd than in China. We all know every family in China cannot own two cars, a television, a computer and eat at Macdonald's and Pizza Hut. The Chinese people are being sold an impossible, huge lie. The world's resources simply cannot support that level of economic expansion. But notice how the Western capitalists lick at the teat of China, desperate for the masturbatory image of limitless markets with no regard to human rights. Lu Sun foresaw it all and conveys it along with Kafka: how the hugeness of this compelling country becomes a sort of mysterious absolute.

The Outsider (1942) by Albert Camus. Still as valid as ever, Camus's pellucid first novel is a relentless attack on the lies and hypocrisy of our Europe and what we dare to call justice. Mersault's story will be as deeply moving in the next century as in this one if we continue to feel simple joys and if we continue to believe in a human justice and the abolition of the death sentence. We need to read it and *live* more urgently than ever. Mersault is guilty of a spontaneous and horrible murder, but if we read the book carefully, we see he is really sentenced to death because he sleeps with Marie the day after his mother's funeral, rather than for the murder. With the insane forces of society against him, Mersault really does rise to the stature of what Camus intended, the only Christ we deserve in this or any other century. We move into the twenty-first century but still our society is deeply anti-human. We refuse to reform society on utilitarian grounds or admit the finite joys of the moment but continue to live and to kill for abstractions. Basically we still haven't faced up to death. The wonderful millennium – but what is there to celebrate? Genocide is back in Europe and The Bill of Human Rights is popular toilet paper. We've learned nothing from Camus.

The Atrocity Exhibition (1970) by J. G. Ballard. Almost thirty years old but still reading as if it was published yesterday, Ballard's *The Atrocity Exhibition* is the only self-consciously 'futuristic' work I've included in my top-ten classics for the twenty-first century, though I don't think Ballard himself would consider his *oeuvre* at all futuristic. Stunning in that Ballard is close to Kafka. Rather than concentrate on the hardware of the future, Ballard has always looked inwards, to the effects of the twentieth-century technology on the individual human psyche, on our feverish dreams, our fears and sexuality. He is so ahead of his time he will be a laureate of the twenty-first century.

Wuthering Heights (1847) by Emily Brontë. The antidote to Shakespeare's sonnets: your offspring does *not* ennoble you! What a mysterious and frightening novel! The heroine is dead even less than half-way in and the story revolves around the terrible destructive consequences of passionate love. Like Gogol and Beckett, this novel threatens the traditional novelist's omnipotence by questioning the distorted recollections of the narrator. She was doing things in this novel that so-called Post Moderns haven't even discovered yet. Emily's dead in heaven before we're even born.

All About H. Hatterr (1948) by G. V. Desani. A real lost masterpiece; this novel is sort of Flann O'Brien meets the Anglo-Indian mind! Hilarious, linguistically runaway and sometimes plain bewildering, the book never gets the status granted to say Forster, despite its fans, who've included T. S. Eliot, Anthony Burgess and Salman Rushdie. Too intelligent and subversive by half in his stereotype-busting gusto, Desani forged something truly creative in his language. Out of the India-meets-the-West ferment, which for me, has produced in Indian writers too polite and formal a prose style, Desani's vigorous originality towers above. The book is, disgracefully, out of print.

Fishboy (1993) by Mark Richard. An inbred cousin-cross between

Cormac McCarthy and *Moby Dick*, this phantasm of a novel is told from a ghost's point of view, a ghost bred out of chemical spillage and reared by rats and snakes. Fishboy works as a cook aboard a demented fishing trawler! For its mastery of prose alone it will be worth reading in one hundred years time. Richard's imagination seems as deep and ceaseless as the sea itself as he takes us on a bastard voyage aboard a contemporary equivalent of the Pequod. It's as if all the grandest freaks and bad trips of the American South have been pushed offshore aboard this inspired novel. I tried to choose between this and *Moby Dick* and came away with this.

The Jerry Cornelius Quartet: The Final Programme, A Cure for Cancer, The English Assassin and *The Condition of Musak* (1965–1976) by Michael Moorcock. It seems to me astonishing that Moorcock is not more widely respected in England. This quartet is one of the really worthwhile pieces of English writing of the last thirty years. I suspect Moorcock's rejection from the canon is grounded in his political non-conformism and his admirable feminism. The Quartet is a wondrous thing, a mix of pulp-fiction techniques and comic-magazine culture with literary sophistication and an outraged humanism at the arms trade in the internecine slaughter of the twentieth century. It's all united through Jerry Cornelius – a Jewish cockney and would-be rock star who also happens to be a time traveller – and his family from hell. Jerry is like Dr Who's cheeky nephew. The characterisation is warm and superb and the takes on popular culture are always invigorating. Because of his lack of elitism, no other contemporary English writer seems to capture the moral dilemmas around us with such wry good humour, vigour and style in a richly modernist way.

What are the books you believe should never have been called classics?

I think there are too many fine novels to bother with ones you don't like; it's a very easy game to play and I think, ultimately, novels are so important there shouldn't be time for negativity when so much great fiction is being neglected. But when classic status is claimed for work, you often get astonished at how rotten some of it is. I *will* say that Walter Scott's reputation has always amused me. This old devil was just a hack writer. Admittedly the biggest hack writer of all time. Every sentence in his books has the same rhythm. De da de da de da (comma) de da de da de da (comma) de da de da de da de da de da de da de da (full stop) *ad infinitum*. He just sat there churning this rubbish out night after night. His books are popular with tourists visiting Scotland, though I bet they never finish them after they've got back home. When I was growing up in the Highlands, Menzies newsagent would fill up with every single Scott novel, even the really obscure ones, just before the tourist season kicked off. The only bits of Scott I like are his descriptions of the Waterloo battle site and when he mentions the Illuminati in his introduction to *Waverley*!

I've always thought the status of *Brave New World* and *Nineteen Eighty-four* concealed the astonishing and far greater novel, *We* (1920) by Yevgeny Zamyatin, which has much richer characterisation and becomes more deeply moving because of it. Both Orwell and Huxley borrowed heavily from Zamyatin, but Huxley never admitted that. I think *Nineteen Eight-four* and *Brave New World* have been used as reactionary tools whereas *We* is a far more complex and interesting book. It strikes me as bizarre that *Nineteen Eighty-four* is taught at Eton.

I feel a wee bit guilty about slogging W. Somerset Maugham, because I once won a Somerset Maugham Award, but really! *Cakes and Ale* is painfully written, unintentionally hilarious and really worth reading for its turgid, very English pomposity. Almost surreal in its crapness.

ALAN WARNER *is the author of three novels,* Morvern Callar, These Demented Lands *and* The Sopranos.

Tim Waterstone

What is your definition of a classic?

The booksellers' and publishers' convention used to be that pre-1900 is classic and post-1900 is not. Rather like the division between the collections of the National Gallery and the Tate. Yet later works – *The Forsyte Saga,* for example – now slip through this absurd net and are listed with *Vanity Fair* and the dreadful *Lorna Doone.* It's a muddle, and it's philistine. Drop the term from fiction altogether. I prefer, as a bookseller, to show the whole body of our stock together, quite simply by alphabetical order. What changed the world in the year 1900? Why is that any more significant than, say, the writer's nationality? So put all the W's together. Edith Wharton, Evelyn Waugh, Angus Wilson, Virginia Woolf, H. G. Wells, Hugh Walpole and Mary Wollstonecraft – all together in happy juxtaposition. And throw the classics 'header-boards' in the bin. I've hated the term all my life. From early teenage schooldays – how can English be taught so badly? – spent listening to a bullying Mr Ford snapping his way through a 'classical novelists' course, which succeeded in making even Thackeray dull, and Jane Austen as empty as a Mills and Boon. Thanks to Mr Ford, I've never quite found Jane Austen to this day. D. H. Lawrence I did, though much later, when Mr Ford's successor, bless her, the chaplain's wife on whom for some weeks all my fourteen-year-old erotic fantasies were centred, read with me, entranced, *The Odour of Chrysanthemums,* and, in an epiphany, I understood for the first time that fiction could *mean* something beyond the strictly narrative.

Our questionnaire asks us who at this time is writing with an eye to the twenty-first century? I have no idea. I wouldn't have thought anyone was, apart from the science-fiction people. One has a vague vision of the twenty-first century as a mildly disagreeable place on the whole. Technologically driven, but the trouble is that we've absolutely no idea what that technology will actually comprise. Maybe out there is an Orwell and a *Nineteen Eighty-four* – now *there's* a 'classic' for you. I doubt it. I think we're all looking backwards as a whole. And it doesn't matter that we are. We've had a wonderful century, and of course our best will survive. Who will that be? Roald Dahl, without question. Evelyn Waugh, probably, for his stylistic brilliance. Graham Greene, and I don't care what Anthony Powell has to say to that. Bellow. Updike. Raymond Carver. F. Scott Fitzgerald. Philip Roth. Neither of the Amises. It's our favourite parlour game at home. The tastes of the twenty-first century will be whatever they will be, but Larkin's four-point must-list will be as true then as ever. Could I read it? Did I believe in it? Did I care about it? Would I go on caring about it?

What are your ten essential classic novels for the next 100 years?

Graham Greene's *The End of the Affair*. Such economy, and eroticism, and truth. And the self-pity, of course, which flavours all Greeneland.

F. Scott Fitzgerald's *Tender is the Night*. I believe in it, I care about it, and I go on caring about it. For 'it' read Dick Diver.

Roald Dahl's *Charlie and the Chocolate Factory*. The greatest children's writer ever.

Philip Roth's *American Pastoral*. This is the Great American Novel. And, remarkably, a marvellously sustained portrait of an entirely good man – notoriously the most difficult thing of all for a writer to pull off.

Raymond Carver's *What We Talk About When We Talk About Love*.

Extremely fine writing around the vicissitudes of life at the American fringe in the 1970's.

Evelyn Waugh's *A Handful of Dust*. Waugh's best novel. Bleak, stylish, understated, masterful.

Charles Dickens's *Oliver Twist*. Maudlin as Dickens is at his best, and as rich too in characterisation and narrative as we can expect to find.

Thackeray's *Vanity Fair*. Possibly the best of all nineteenth-century novels, together with . . .

George Eliot's *Middlemarch*. Impeccable: construction, credibility, narrative strength, moral significance all *sans pareil.*

James Joyce's *Ulysses*. Sublime language and imagery and all delivered at a thundering pace.

What are the books you believe should never have been called classics?

All Sir Walter Scott's novels (uncountable). Impenetrable and awful.

TIM WATERSTONE *is a novelist, the founder of Waterstone's and the Chairman of the HMV Media Group.*

Alison Weir

What is your definition of a classic?

What makes a good, classic novel? In my opinion, the main ingredient is a good story well told. That is not as simple as it sounds, and, indeed, many good stories well told do not make classic novels. One of my favourite authors is Barbara Erskine, but I would not describe her wonderful novels as classic, and neither, I think, would she.

A classic novel, therefore, is one that has endured, and will continue to endure, in popularity. It encapsulates the finest kind of writing of the period when it was written, yet has relevance for future generations. It sets a new standard for the future, and has many emulators.

This is, of course, the widest interpretation of the term 'classic', and is probably what most of us understand by it. We do not today make the distinction between the classical literature of the seventeenth and eighteenth centuries and the reactionary romantic writing of the nineteenth: to us, the enduring literary works of both these periods are all classics.

So what defines a classic novel, and how do you tell a good story well? Firstly, you plan your narrative and ensure that it is balanced and well-paced. You define your characters well and portray them as realistic human beings with credible motives and emotions. You employ description to an acceptable degree, to set your scenes and bring your work to life. You make effective use of grammar, punctuation and sentence construction, and use as wide a vocabulary as possible, ensuring that it is relevant to the subject, and avoiding clichés. Finally, and most importantly, you write from the heart, so that the words come leaping onto the page.

But what about the plot, you may ask? Well, that must come from you, and everything to do with that often elusive commodity, inspiration. It is useful, when writing for a commercial market, to have a good knowledge of what is selling well and a sixth-sense for emerging trends. Make sure you have done your research thoroughly, and stick to subjects you know well. Be as original as you can: many of the greatest classical novels were the first of their kind.

I believe that the term 'classic' is useful with regard to literature because it defines the type of novel we should all aspire to read. I am appalled when I read of schools refusing gifts of classic novels for their libraries on the grounds that they are not relevant to the lives of modern children, and I believe that the problem lies with the way in which schools and parents present books to children. If you read good books yourself, and your children see you doing it, they will understand that it is an enjoyable thing to do. If a teacher approaches a classic novel with enthusiasm and understanding, helping pupils to understand it, they will enjoy it and a lifetime of good reading will be established. I took care to introduce my own children to the classics from a very early age, through accessible mediums: we began with the Ladybird Classics series, so that they became familiar with the stories, and they progressed to Shakespeare with *The Animated Tales* around the age of eight. They are now in their teens and have read and enjoyed many of the classics in their original form.

It is the way in which the classics are presented to young people that is crucial. When I announced to my class of not very literary adolescents that we were to be studying *Romeo and Juliet*, the response was a chorus of groans – 'Oh, not Shakespeare!' Yet by the end of the first lesson, they were begging to know what happened next and asking if they could stage a production of the play. When, the following year, we read *Pride and Prejudice*, they panicked over the archaic language, but once they had got used to

it, through careful explanation, they were avid to complete the
book. With *Animal Farm*, once they realised how much more than a
fairy story it was, their enthusiasm knew no bounds.

It was perhaps because I hated the classics at school and only came
to a full appreciation of them in adulthood, that I adopted such a
sympathetic approach to my pupils. From the age of nine, I endured
bowdlerised versions of classic works being read aloud in class, always
by the teacher's favourites, without any clarification or explanation,
and consequently I saw these books – notably *Treasure Island* and *Great
Expectations* – as boring and irrelevant. Even *Jane Eyre*, which I had
loved in its televisual form, became tedious when recited in a
monotone by a fellow pupil. I remember being still resentful in the
Sixth Form, having to read *Sons and Lovers*, which I found utterly
disturbing. By then, I had myself chosen to study English at A-level,
having become inspired by a growing love of history and a
consequent passion for Shakespeare and Chaucer, yet I hated the
arbitrary selection of the books on the syllabus. *Middlemarch* I found
stifling, and still do. Yet my private reading included Boccaccio's
Decameron, Smollett's *Humphry Clinker*, and *Wuthering Heights*.

There are many authors today who are obviously writing with an
eye to the twenty-first century, although I have to say that I do not
read many of their books because the subjects bore me. I will come
clean now and say that I am no fan of the modern novel. However, I
make exceptions: I loved *Birdsong* by Sebastian Faulks, because I
found it so moving, and I appreciate that many books are well written.
But we read for enjoyment, and I can only deplore the fact that the
historical novel, my favourite genre, has gone out of fashion.
Fortunately, there are signs, with the reissue of Anya Seton's books
and *Young Bess* by Margaret Irwin, that a revival is on its way.

I think that the qualities a novel will need to assure readership in
the twenty-first century are the same that it needs now, which I have
outlined above. Fashions in novels go in cycles, and there is no
doubt that this will continue in the next century. A certain
readership will always expect modernity and a fresh approach, yet
the books that are borrowed again and again from libraries, as

anyone can see, are family sagas (oh, not again!), historical novels, detective fiction, science fiction, horror fiction and stories of the supernatural. Will Jean Plaidy and Barbara Cartland endure as Jane Austen has? One would think not, but their popularity shows little sign of abating.

No, I don't read Jean Plaidy or Barbara Cartland, but I can hear the howls of derision from the literary intelligentsia at my mere mention of them. I confess, however, that, when it comes to choosing ten essential classic novels for the twenty-first century – a horrendous task – I have found I am not interested in opting for the kind of books that win the Booker Prize. I would love to say I was as enthralled by *Captain Corelli's Mandolin* as everyone else, but I abandoned it in boredom after persevering for 160 pages. It just did not appeal to me.

And there we come to the crux of the matter. There might be great snobbery in literary circles when it comes to the novel, but when it comes down to it we read what we enjoy, and it's nobody's business but our own. And that is why my list is going to be deliberately reactionary (in parts)!!! Here it is, then, Alison Weir's ten essential classic novels for the twenty-first century . . .

What are your ten essential classic novels for the next 100 years?

Norah Lofts's trilogy, *The Town House, The House at Old Vine* and *The House at Sunset*. I have read this series again and again since the Sixties and each time I obtain fresh enjoyment from it. The story is utterly compelling and well-paced, the characters alarmingly real and the detail authentic, while Lofts employs innuendo to hint at things better left unsaid. Which just goes to prove that something left to the imagination is far more effective than pages of lurid and gory detail.

Anya Seton's *Katherine*. A classic historical novel, so well researched and written and it deserves to be hailed as the best of its genre. I would, in fact, recommend any of her books.

Jane Austen's *Pride and Prejudice*. A wonderful tale of manners and relationships that has an appeal for every generation. Need I say more?

Daphne du Maurier's *Rebecca*. One of the most haunting and beautifully written books of the twentieth century, its enduring appeal has been enhanced by one of Alfred Hitchcock's best films and two very vivid television dramatisations.

Sebastian Faulks's *Birdsong*. Although I found the love story unconvincing, Faulks's vivid and poignant portrayal of the Great War and the men who fought in it renders this gripping book a masterpiece.

Sir Arthur Conan Doyle's *The Complete Sherlock Holmes Stories* – the greatest of all detective novels.

Charlotte Brontë's *Jane Eyre*. The romantic Gothic novel at its best: a wonderful story of tragedy, mystery and love.

Emily Brontë's *Wuthering Heights*. Brontë's portrayal of Heathcliff is remarkable given the fact that she was a spinster living in a remote area, which goes to prove how powerful the imagination can be. The convoluted structure of the novel makes it demanding to read, but is ultimately very effective.

D. H. Lawrence's *Lady Chatterley's Lover*. Forget the scandal that once surrounded this book, it is a brilliantly conceived and well-written portrayal of the class divisions that prevailed in the Twenties, and its characters are disturbingly real. The sex scenes seem tame by late-twentieth-century standards, yet are skilfully handled. Altogether a riveting read.

Susan Hill's *The Woman in Black*. I would have liked to nominate the stories of M. R. James, but they cannot be described as novels. Susan Hill has written this masterpiece in the tradition of M. R. James, and it is brilliant. I found it more chilling on the second reading, and it really is one of the most convincing ghost stories. Its successful adaptation to the stage will doubtless ensure its enduring popularity.

What are the books you believe should never have been called classics?

I am unable to list any classic novels that I believe should never have been called classics because they have endured as such and therefore they are classics. Whether I like them or not is beside the point. For example, I find most of the works of the Bloomsbury group tedious, but I cannot say they should never have been called classics because, clearly, there is that in them that gives them a wide appeal.

Having said that, could somebody please assure me that Virginia Woolf's mind-numbing *To the Lighthouse*, which I was forced to read at school, will never again be called a classic!

ALISON WEIR *is a historian. Her books include* The Six Wives of Henry VIII, Children of England *and* Elizabeth the Queen.

Chris Woodhead

What is your definition of a classic?

A classic novel is a novel that has stood the test of time – by which I mean, if we are to be certain, at least fifty, and probably a hundred or more years. I have no difficulty with the concept of a 'classic'. Some novels are better than others. Classics are simply the best. A classic novel sets the individual life within the wider context of a society and its history. This is the essential test and as Iris Murdoch once pointed out, in what has become a classic essay, most twentieth-century novels are either 'crystalline or journalistic'. They do not pass the essential test.

I did not feel that I was forced to read classic texts at school. As a young child, I progressed from fairy tales to Biggles with a great deal of pleasure. There were times at secondary school when the detailed textual analysis of novels which struck me as irrelevant and over-valued left me cold. But then, in my O-level year, I read, initially with some reluctance, *Wuthering Heights*, and I realised the impact great literature could have.

What are your ten essential classic novels for the next 100 years?

Nineteenth-century novels like *Anna Karenina, War and Peace, The Brothers Karamazov, Emma, Middlemarch* and *Our Mutual Friend* are classic classics and will (or ought to be) on everybody's lists. If we take the inclusion of such novels for granted and focus on more recent and, therefore, more controversial and interesting possibilities, my list would certainly include:

The Rainbow and *Women in Love* by D. H. Lawrence, because in Frank Kermode's words: 'Decadence and renovation, death and rebirth, in the last days, are hard to tell apart, being caught up in the terrors.'

A Dance to the Music of Time by Anthony Powell, because no twentieth-century novel more obviously passes Iris Murdoch's test: this is our history, our society.

The Spire by William Golding, because whilst it was written only thirty-four years ago and is obviously very much a crystalline fable, it speaks powerfully and eloquently and movingly to anyone who is driven to achieve anything.

Wolf Solent by John Cowper Powys, because, 'comic King Lear' that he is, Wolf's sexual, domestic and metaphysical dilemmas resonate all too strongly.

The Tree of Man by Patrick White, because in drawing us into the lives of its characters it captures a moment in Australian history, and has, like *Voss,* an extraordinary mythic quality.

The Portrait of a Lady by Henry James, because of chapter 42.

A Word Child by Iris Murdoch because Hilary Burde, travelling the Circle Line, is so much a figure of our egotistic times that I am prepared to break, once again, my chronological rule.

A Burnt-out Case by Graham Greene, because no twentieth-century novelist has written more movingly of the search for meaning in a world without faith.

Heart of Darkness by Joseph Conrad, because it exposes the danger of idealism.

The Untouchable by John Banville, because this is the greatest work so far by the best and most intelligent contemporary novelist writing today.

What are the books you believe should never have been called classics?

I am not prepared to list books that I think should never have been given classic status. There are books I have struggled with (such as *Ulysses*, *Mrs Dalloway* and *Remembrance of Things Past*), but I am hopeful that at some point I will grow up sufficiently to appreciate their (to me, thus far) mysterious charms.

CHRIS WOODHEAD *is Her Majesty's Chief Inspector of Schools.*

The Lists

21st-century Classics

Our contributors' selection of essential classics for the next 100 years.

Arrow of God
Chinua Achebe

Things Fall Apart
Chinua Achebe

Watership Down
Richard Adams

Lucky Jim
Kingsley Amis

London Fields
Martin Amis

Money
Martin Amis

Time's Arrow
Martin Amis

The Bridge over the Drina
Ivo Andric

Epitaph of a Small Winner
Machado de Assis

The Robber Bride
Margaret Atwood

Emma
Jane Austen

Pride and Prejudice
Jane Austen

Moon Palace
Paul Auster

The New York Trilogy
Paul Auster

The Birthday Boys
Beryl Bainbridge

The Atrocity Exhibition
J. G. Ballard

Empire of the Sun
J. G. Ballard

The Voices of Time
J. G. Ballard

La Cousine Bette
Honoré de Balzac

Lost Illusions
Honoré de Balzac

Athena
John Banville

The Untouchable
John Banville

The Regeneration Trilogy
Pat Barker

The Molloy Trilogy
Samuel Beckett

Watt
Samuel Beckett

Herzog
Saul Bellow

Petersburg
Andrei Bely

The War of Don Emmanuel's Nether Parts
Louis de Bernières

The Stars My Destination
Alfred Bester

The Heat of the Day
Elizabeth Bowen

Station to Station lyrics
David Bowie

The Martian Chronicles
Ray Bradbury

The Tenant of Wildfell Hall
Anne Brontë

Jane Eyre
Charlotte Brontë

Wuthering Heights
Emily Brontë

Jampot Smith
Jeremy Brooks

Magnus
George Mackay Brown

Smallcreep's Day
Peter C. Brown

The Story of Babar, the Little Elephant
Jean de Brunhoff

Ambition
Julie Burchill

Earthly Powers
Anthony Burgess

Evelina
Fanny Burney

The Naked Lunch
William Burroughs

The Way of All Flesh
Samuel Butler

Possession
A. S. Byatt

Invisible Cities
Italo Calvino

The Outsider
Albert Camus

Axel
Bo Carpelan

Explosion in a Cathedral
Alejo Carpentier

Alice's Adventures in Wonderland
Lewis Carroll

*Through the Looking-Glass and
    What Alice Found There*
Lewis Carroll

The Magic Toyshop
Angela Carter

Nights at the Circus
Angela Carter

Wise Children
Angela Carter

*What We Talk About When We
    Talk About Love*
Raymond Carver

O Pioneers!
Willa Cather

Don Quixote
Cervantes

The Big Sleep
Raymond Chandler

Oh What a Paradise It Seems
John Cheever

The Pale Horse
Agatha Christie

What a Carve-Up!
Jonathan Coe

The Life and Times of Michael K
J. M. Coetzee

The Vision of the Fool
Cecil Collins

The Moonstone
Wilkie Collins

The Woman in White
Wilkie Collins

Manservant and Maidservant
Ivy Compton-Burnett

The Heart of Darkness
Joseph Conrad

Nostromo
Joseph Conrad

The Collected Poems
e e cummings

Victory
Joseph Conrad

Charlie and the Chocolate Factory
Roald Dahl

What's Bred in the Bone
Robertson Davies

Reading in the Dark
Seamus Deane

Robinson Crusoe
Daniel Defoe

The Names
Don DeLillo

White Noise
Don DeLillo

All About H. Hatterr
G. V. Desani

The Three Stigmata of Palmer Eldritch
Philip K. Dick

Bleak House
Charles Dickens

David Copperfield
Charles Dickens

Great Expectations
Charles Dickens

Little Dorrit
Charles Dickens

Oliver Twist
Charles Dickens

Is This Allowed?
William Donaldson

The Brothers Karamazov
Fyodor Dostoevsky

Crime and Punishment
Fyodor Dostoevsky

The Idiot
Fyodor Dostoevsky

The Complete Sherlock Holmes Stories
Sir Arthur Conan Doyle

The Van
Roddy Doyle

The Lover
Marguerite Duras

The Alexandria Quartet
Lawrence Durrell

Mercy
Andrea Dworkin

The Name of the Rose
Umberto Eco

St Agnes's Stand
Thomas Eidson

Daniel Deronda
George Eliot

Middlemarch
George Eliot

The Mill on the Floss
George Eliot

Absalom, Absalom!
William Faulkner

Birdsong
Sebastian Faulks

Bridget Jones's Diary
Helen Fielding

Tom Jones
Henry Fielding

The Blue Flower
Penelope Fitzgerald

The Great Gatsby
F. Scott Fitzgerald

Tender is the Night
F. Scott Fitzgerald

Madame Bovary
Gustave Flaubert

A Man Could Stand Up
Ford Madox Ford

The Sportswriter
Richard Ford

Namedropper
Emma Forrest

Howard's End
E. M. Forster

A Passage to India
E. M. Forster

Have the Men Had Enough?
Margaret Forster

The Day of the Jackal
Frederick Forsyth

The Magus
John Fowles

Cold Mountain
Charles Frazier

The Women's Room
Marilyn French

Cranford
Mrs Gaskell

Cold Comfort Farm
Stella Gibbons

The Sorrows of Young Werther
Goethe

Lord of the Flies
William Golding

The Spire
William Golding

The Vicar of Wakefield
Oliver Goldsmith

My Son's Story
Nadine Gordimer

The Wind in the Willows
Kenneth Grahame

The Tin Drum
Gunter Grass

I, Claudius
Robert Graves

Lanark
Alasdair Gray

Brighton Rock
Graham Greene

A Burnt-out Case
Graham Greene

The End of the Affair
Graham Greene

The Human Factor
Graham Greene

The Power and the Glory
Graham Greene

See Under: Love
David Grossman

The Diary of a Nobody
George and Weedon Grossmith

The Silver Darlings
Neil Gunn

Hangover Square
Patrick Hamilton

Jude the Obscure
Thomas Hardy

Tess of the D'Urbervilles
Thomas Hardy

Catch-22
Joseph Heller

Something Happened
Joseph Heller

A Farewell to Arms
Ernest Hemingway

For Whom the Bell Tolls
Ernest Hemingway

The Tintin Books
Hergé

The Woman in Black
Susan Hill

*Private Memoirs and Confessions of
    a Justified Sinner*
James Hogg

About a Boy
Nick Hornby

Les Misérables
Victor Hugo

Brave New World
Aldous Huxley

The Cider House Rules
John Irving

A Prayer for Owen Meany
John Irving

The Remains of the Day
Kazuo Ishiguro

The Prince of West End Avenue
Alan Isler

The Ambassadors
Henry James

The Portrait of a Lady
Henry James

Three Men in a Boat
Jerome K. Jerome

Albert Angelo
B. S. Johnson

Dubliners
James Joyce

Finnegans Wake
James Joyce

*A Portrait of the Artist as a Young
    Man*
James Joyce

Ulysses
James Joyce

The Castle
Franz Kafka

The Trial
Franz Kafka

Fowler's End
Gerald Kersh

One Flew Over the Cuckoo's Nest
Ken Kesey

The White Bird Passes
Jessie Kesson

Pet Sematary
Stephen King

Darkness at Noon
Arthur Koestler

The Painted Bird
Jerzy Kosinski

The Unbearable Lightness of Being
Milan Kundera

The Stone Angel
Margaret Laurence

Lady Chatterley's Lover
D. H. Lawrence

The Rainbow
D. H. Lawrence

Sons and Lovers
D. H. Lawrence

Women in Love
D. H. Lawrence

*As I Walked Out One Midsummer
    Morning*
Laurie Lee

Cider with Rosie
Laurie Lee

The X-Men
Stan Lee

Stick
Elmore Leonard

The Golden Notebook
Doris Lessing

The Periodic Table
Primo Levi

*The Lion, the Witch and the
    Wardrobe*
C. S. Lewis

That Hideous Strength
C. S. Lewis

The Magic Pudding
Norman Lindsay

Small World
David Lodge

*The Town House; The House at Old
   Vine; The House at Sunset*
Nora Lofts

Gentlemen Prefer Blondes
Anita Loos

All the Pretty Horses
Cormac McCarthy

Blood Meridian
Cormac McCarthy

The Heart is a Lonely Hunter
Carson McCullers

England, Their England
A. G. McDonnell

Enduring Love
Ian McEwan

The Story of My Life
Jay McInerney

Dunedin
Shena Mackay

Redhill Rococo
Shena Mackay

The Executioner's Song
Norman Mailer

The Magic Mountain
Thomas Mann

One Hundred Years of Solitude
Gabriel Garcia Marquez

I Am Legend
Richard Matheson

The Razor's Edge
W Somerset Maugham

Rebecca
Daphne du Maurier

Moby Dick
Herman Melville

Fugitive Pieces
Anne Michaels

Tropic of Cancer
Henry Miller

The House at Pooh Corner
A. A. Milne

Winnie-the-Pooh
A. A. Milne

Paradise Lost
John Milton

The Jerry Cornelius Quartet
Michael Moorcock

Anagrams
Lorrie Moore

The Tale of Genji
Lady Murasaki

A Severed Head
Iris Murdoch

A Word Child
Iris Murdoch

The Man Without Qualities
Robert Musil

Lolita
Vladimir Nabokov

Pale Fire
Vladimir Nabokov

A Bend in the River
V. S. Naipaul

The Enigma of Arrival
V. S. Naipaul

A House for Mr Biswas
V. S. Naipaul

The Magic City
E. Nesbit

Clever Bill
William Nicholson

As Good as it Gets
Simon Nolan

The Third Policeman
Flann O'Brien

*A Trail of Heart's Blood Wherever
  We Go*
Robert Olmstead

The English Patient
Michael Ondaatje

The Shipyard
Juan Carlos Onetti

Animal Farm
George Orwell

Keep the Aspidistra Flying
George Orwell

Nineteen Eighty-four
George Orwell

U.S.A.
John Dos Passos

The Gormenghast Trilogy
Mervyn Peake

Life: A User's Manual
George Perec

A Demon in My View
Edgar Allan Poe

A Dance to the Music of Time
Anthony Powell

Wolf Solent
John Cowper Powys

À la Recherche du Temps Perdu
Marcel Proust

Gravity's Rainbow
Thomas Pynchon

Mary Plain books
Gwyneth Rae

Wide Sargasso Sea
Jean Rhys

An Invisible Memory
Joao Ubaldo Ribeiro

Fishboy
Mark Richard

Clarissa
Samuel Richardson

Pavane
Keith Roberts

*The Devil to Pay in the
    Backlands*
Joao Guimareas Rosa

American Pastoral
Philip Roth

Portnoy's Complaint
Philip Roth

Sabbath's Theater
Philip Roth

Midnight's Children
Salman Rushdie

The Satanic Verses
Salman Rushdie

Shame
Salman Rushdie

The Catcher in the Rye
J. D. Salinger

Taxi Driver
Paul Schrader

The Raj Quartet
Paul Scott

A Suitable Boy
Vikram Seth

Katherine
Anya Seton

Frankenstein
Mary Shelley

The Last Man
Mary Shelley

Larry's Party
Carol Shields

And Quiet Flows the Don
Mikhail Sholokhov

The Georgics
Claude Simon

Downriver
Iain Sinclair

A Thousand Acres
Jane Smiley

The Expedition of Humphry Clinker
Tobias Smollett

The Conscience of the Rich
C. P. Snow

Sophie's Choice
William Styron

The Cancer Ward
Alexander Solzhenitsyn

The True Story of Ah-Q
Lu Sun

A Far Cry from Kensington
Muriel Spark

Last Orders
Graham Swift

Loitering with Intent
Muriel Spark

Waterland
Graham Swift

The Grapes of Wrath
John Steinbeck

Gulliver's Travels
Jonathan Swift

Of Mice and Men
John Steinbeck

A Secret History
Donna Tartt

The Charterhouse of Parma
Stendhal

Vanity Fair
William Thackeray

Scarlet and Black
Stendhal

The Tourist
Matt Thorne

Tristram Shandy
Laurence Sterne

The Hobbit
J. R. R. Tolkien

Dr Jekyll and Mr Hyde
Robert Louis Stevenson

The Lord of the Rings
J. R. R. Tolkien

Treasure Island
Robert Louis Stevenson

Anna Karenina
Leo Tolstoy

A Flag for Sunrise
Robert Stone

War and Peace
Leo Tolstoy

Radcliffe
David Storey

The Erl-King
Michel Tournier

One Last Embrace
Jack Trevor Story

Felicia's Journey
William Trevor

Phineas Finn
Anthony Trollope

The Small House at Allington
Anthony Trollope

Huckleberry Finn
Mark Twain

Dinner at the Homesick Restaurant
Anne Tyler

Kristin Lavransdatter
Sigrid Undset

Rabbit at Rest
John Updike

Player Piano
Kurt Vonnegut

Slaughterhouse 5
Kurt Vonnegut

Infinite Jest
David Foster Wallace

Jambo
Dave Ward

Morvern Callar
Alan Warner

The True Heart
Sylvia Townsend Warner

Brideshead Revisited
Evelyn Waugh

A Handful of Dust
Evelyn Waugh

The Loved One
Evelyn Waugh

The Sword of Honor Trilogy
Evelyn Waugh

The History of Mr Polly
H. G. Wells

Trainspotting
Irvine Welsh

The Age of Innocence
Edith Wharton

The Tree of Man
Patrick White

The Vivisector
Patrick White

The Once and Future King
T. H. White

The Picture of Dorian Gray
Oscar Wilde

Suddenly, Last Summer
Tennessee Williams

Anglo-Saxon Attitudes
Angus Wilson

No Laughing Matter
Angus Wilson

Oranges are not the Only Fruit
Jeanette Winterson

Look Homeward Angel
Thomas Wolfe

The Right Stuff
Tom Wolfe

Memoirs of Hadrian
Marguerite Yourcenar

Mrs Dalloway
Virginia Woolf

Germinal
Emile Zola

To the Lighthouse
Virginia Woolf

Some authors were nominated for some or all of their work:

Martin Amis
Paul Auster
Saul Bellow
John Braine
Joseph Conrad
Daniel Defoe
Charles Dickens
George Eliot
Henry Fielding
E. M. Forster
John Fowles
Nadine Gordimer
Thomas Hardy
Ernest Hemingway
Henry James
James Joyce
D. H. Lawrence

Doris Lessing
Herman Melville
Iris Murdoch
R. K. Narayan
Barbara Pym
Mordecai Richler
Philip Roth
Tobias Smollett
Muriel Spark
Robert Louis Stevenson
William Thackeray
William Trevor
Anthony Trollope
John Updike
Evelyn Waugh
Patrick White

Disputed Classics

The books and authors that contributors felt didn't merit the term 'classic'.

Watership Down
Richard Adams

Lucky Jim
Kingsley Amis

Mansfield Park
Jane Austen

Another Country
James Baldwin

The Mezzanine
Nicholson Baker

Union Street
Pat Barker

Peter Pan in Kensington Gardens
J. M. Barrie

Beowulf

G
John Berger

Wuthering Heights
Emily Brontë

The Thirty-nine Steps
John Buchan

The Last Days of Pompeii
Edward Bulwer-Lytton

The Pilgrim's Progress
John Bunyan

Don Quixote
Cervantes

Who Killed Roger Ackroyd?
Agatha Christie

The Heart of Darkness
Joseph Conrad

Nostromo
Joseph Conrad

Moll Flanders
Daniel Defoe

Sybil
Benjamin Disraeli

Foucault's Pendulum
Umberto Eco

Daniel Deronda
George Eliot

Silas Marner
George Eliot

Tom Jones
Henry Fielding

The Great Gatsby
F. Scott Fitzgerald

Tender is the Night
F. Scott Fitzgerald

Howard's End
E. M. Forster

The Forsyte Saga
John Galsworthy

Corydon
Aldous Huxley

The Counterfeiters
André Gide

Caleb Williams
William Godwin

Lord of the Flies
William Golding

The Well of Loneliness
Radclyffe Hall

Jude the Obscure
Thomas Hardy

The Mayor of Casterbridge
Thomas Hardy

A Farewell to Arms
Ernest Hemingway

For Whom the Bell Tolls
Ernest Hemingway

The Old Man and the Sea
Ernest Hemingway

A Shropshire Lad
A. E. Housman

Far Away and Long Ago
W. H. Hudson

Brave New Word
Aldous Husley

The Ambassadors
Henry James

The Golden Bowl
Henry James

The Portrait of a Lady
Henry James

Rasselas
Samuel Johnson

Finnegans Wake
James Joyce

Ulysses
James Joyce

How Late it Was, How Late
James Kelman

On the Road
Jack Kerouac

Westward Ho!
Charles Kingsley

The Jungle Book
Rudyard Kipling

Lady Chatterley's Lover
D. H. Lawrence

The Rainbow
D. H. Lawrence

Sons and Lovers
D. H. Lawrence

Women in Love
D. H. Lawrence

Cider with Rosie
Laurie Lee

The Narnia Books
C. S. Lewis

Under the Volcano
Malcolm Lowry

Moby Dick
Herman Melville

The Egoist
George Meredith

Sexus
Henry Miller

The House at Pooh Corner
A. A. Milne

Gone with the Wind
Margaret Mitchell

Lolita
Vladimir Nabokov

Animal Farm
George Orwell

Nineteen Eighty-four
George Orwell

A Dance to the Music of Time
Anthony Powell

Vineland
Thomas Pynchon

Pamela
Samuel Richardson

Clarissa
Samuel Richardson

Portnoy's Complaint
Philip Roth

The Moor's Last Sigh
Salman Rushdie

The Little Prince
Antoine de Saint-Exupéry

The Catcher in the Rye
J. D. Salinger

The Age of Reason Trilogy
Jean-Paul Sartre

Nausea
Jean-Paul Sartre

Ivanhoe
Walter Scott

Quentin Durward Walter Scott	*The Colour Purple* Alice Walker
Waverley Walter Scott	*Robert Elsmere* Mrs Humphry Ward
Last Exit to Brooklyn Hubert Selby Jnr.	*Anna Veronica* H. G. Wells
Uncle Tom's Cabin Harriet Beecher Stowe	*The Bonfire of the Vanities* Tom Wolfe
Vanity Fair William Thackeray	*To the Lighthouse* Virginia Woolf
The Lord of the Rings J. R. R. Tolkien	*The Waves* Virginia Woolf
Around the World in Eighty Days Jules Verne	

Some authors were nominated for some or all of their work:

Kingsley Amis
Martin Amis
Jane Austen
Charles Dickens
Fyodor Dostoevsky
T. S. Eliot
Ian Fleming
Dick Francis
D. H. Lawrence
Norman Mailer
George Meredith
Charles Morgan
George Orwell

Thomas Pynchon
Philip Roth
Walter Scott
Alfred, Lord Tennyson
Anthony Trollope
Horace Walpole
Mary Webb
Angus Wilson
Jeanette Winterson
Virginia Woolf
William Wordsworth
Emile Zola

The Books of the Century

The results of the Waterstone's 1997 national poll of readers, conducted in association with Channel 4.

1. *The Lord of the Rings*
   J. R. R. Tolkien

2. *Nineteen Eighty-four*
   George Orwell

3. *Animal Farm*
   George Orwell

4. *Ulysses*
   James Joyce

5. *Catch-22*
   Joseph Heller

6. *The Catcher in the Rye*
   J. D. Salinger

7. *To Kill a Mockingbird*
   Harper Lee

8. *One Hundred Years of Solitude*
   Gabriel Garcia Marquez

9. *The Grapes of Wrath*
   John Steinbeck

10. *Trainspotting*
    Irvine Welsh

11. *Wild Swans*
    Jung Chang

12. *The Great Gatsby*
    F. Scott Fitzgerald

13. *Lord of the Flies*
    William Golding

14. *On the Road*
    Jack Kerouac

15. *Brave New World*
    Aldous Huxley

16. *The Wind in the Willows*
    Kenneth Grahame

17. *Winnie-the-Pooh*
    A. A. Milne

18. *The Colour Purple*
    Alice Walker

19. The Hobbit
J. R. R. Tolkien

20. The Outsider
Albert Camus

21. The Lion, the Witch and the Wardrobe
C. S. Lewis

22. The Trial
Franz Kafka

23. Gone with the Wind
Margaret Mitchell

24. The Hitchhiker's Guide to the Galaxy
Douglas Adams

25. Midnight's Children
Salman Rushdie

26. The Diary of Anne Frank
Anne Frank

27. A Clockwork Orange
Anthony Burgess

28. Sons and Lovers
D. H. Lawrence

29. To the Lighthouse
Virginia Woolf

30. If This is a Man
Primo Levi

31. Lolita
Vladimir Nabokov

32. The Wasp Factory
Iain Banks

33. Remembrance of Things Past
Marcel Proust

34. Charlie and the Chocolate Factory
Roald Dahl

35. Of Mice and Men
John Steinbeck

36. Beloved
Toni Morrison

37. Possession
A. S. Byatt

38. Heart of Darkness
Joseph Conrad

39. A Passage to India
E. M. Forster

40. Watership Down
Richard Adams

41. Sophie's World
Jostein Gaarder

42. The Name of the Rose
Umberto Eco

43. Love in the Time of Cholera
Gabriel Garcia Marquez

44. Rebecca
Daphne du Maurier

45. *The Remains of the Day*
    Kazuo Ishiguro

46. *The Unbearable Lightness of Being*
    Milan Kundera

47. *Birdsong*
    Sebastian Faulks

48. *Howard's Way*
    E. M. Forster

49. *Brideshead Revisited*
    Evelyn Waugh

50. *A Suitable Boy*
    Vikram Seth

51. *Dune*
    Frank Herbert

52. *A Prayer for Owen Meany*
    John Irving

53. *Perfume*
    Patrick Suskind

54. *Doctor Zhivago*
    Boris Pasternak

55. *The Gormenghast Trilogy*
    Mervyn Peake

56. *Cider with Rosie*
    Laurie Lee

57. *The Bell Jar*
    Sylvia Plath

58. *The Handmaid's Tale*
    Margaret Atwood

59. *Testament of Youth*
    Vera Brittain

60. *The Magus*
    John Fowles

61. *Brighton Rock*
    Graham Greene

62. *The Ragged-trousered Philanthropists*
    Robert Tressell

63. *The Master and Margarita*
    Mikhail Bulgakov

64. *Tales of the City*
    Armistead Maupin

65. *The French Lieutenant's Woman*
    John Fowles

66. *Captain Corelli's Mandolin*
    Louis de Bernières

67. *Slaughterhouse 5*
    Kurt Vonnegut

68. *Zen and the Art of Motorcycle Maintenance*
    Robert Pirsig

69. *A Room with a View*
    E. M. Forster

70. *Lucky Jim*
    Kingsley Amis

71. *It*
    Stephen King

72. *The Power and the Glory*
    Graham Greene

73. *The Stand*
    Stephen King

74. *All Quiet on the Western Front*
    Erich Maria Remarque

75. *Paddy Clarke Ha Ha Ha*
    Roddy Doyle

76. *Matilda*
    Roald Dahl

77. *American Psycho*
    Bret Easton Ellis

78. *Fear and Loathing in Las Vegas*
    Hunter S. Thompson

79. *A Brief History of Time*
    Stephen Hawking

80. *James and the Giant Peach*
    Roald Dahl

81. *Lady Chatterley's Lover*
    D. H. Lawrence

82. *The Bonfire of the Vanities*
    Tom Wolfe

83. *Complete Cookery Course*
    Delia Smith

84. *An Evil Cradling*
    Brian Keenan

85. *The Rainbow*
    D. H Lawrence

86. *Down and Out in Paris and
    London*
    George Orwell

87. *2001: A Space Odyssey*
    Arthur C. Clarke

88. *The Tin Drum*
    Gunter Grass

89. *One Day in the Life of Ivan
    Denisovich*
    Alexander Solzhenitsyn

90. *A Long Walk to Freedom*
    Nelson Mandela

91. *The Selfish Gene*
    Richard Dawkins

92. *Jurassic Park*
    Michael Crichton

93. *The Alexandria Quartet*
    Lawrence Durrell

94. *Crys, the Beloved Country*
    Alan Paton

95. *High Fidelity*
    Nick Hornby

96. *The Van*
    Roddy Doyle

97. *The BFG*
    Roald Dahl

98. *Earthly Powers*
    Anthony Burgess

99. *I, Claudius*
    Robert Graves

100. *The Horse Whisperer*
     Nicholas Evans